A ReefBum's Guide To Keeping an SPS Reef Tank

A Blueprint For Success

By Keith Berkelhamer

A ReefBum's Guide To Keeping an SPS Reef Tank:
A Blueprint For Success
by Keith Berkelhamer

Published by ReefBum, LLC
237 Stony Hill Road
Warren, Vermont 05674
https://reefbum.com

Printed in the United States of America
First Printing: 2017

Copyright © 2017 ReefBum

All rights reserved. This book or any portion thereof may not be reproduced or used in any manner whatsoever without the express written permission of the publisher except for the use of brief quotations in a book review. For permissions contact:

info@reefbum.com

Editor: Courtney Jenkins

ISBN: 9781981248605

TABLE OF CONTENTS

Acknowledgements 6

CHAPTER ONE 8

Introduction 8
How I Became a ReefBum 8

CHAPTER 2 13

Reefology 101 13
Knowledge is Power 14
Patience is a Virtue 16
Resist The Urge to Submerge 18
The KISS Principle of Reef Keeping 20

CHAPTER 3 22

Equipment & Filtration 22
Choosing The Right Aquarium 22
Sumps 33
Remote Sumps 34
Connecting the Tank to the Sump: Designing a Plumbing Roadmap 39
Lighting: My Success With Metal Halides 46
Calcium and Alkalinity Supplementation 48
Go With The Flow: Why Strong Circulation is Important for SPS 51
Skimmers 53
A UV Sterilizer For a Reef Tank? 58
Filtration 61
Chillers 65
Aquarium Controllers 67

CHAPTER 4 70

Aquascaping 70
Less is Better 70
Dry Rock vs Live Rock – Which One to Choose? 73
Sand Bed or Bare Bottom? 75

CHAPTER 5 78

Bringing a Tank to Life 78
Cycling a Tank – Live Rock 78
Cycling a Tank – Dry Rock 85
Introducing Fish and Corals 86
Time is On Your Side: Go Slow When Adding Livestock 89

CHAPTER 6 92

Fish Stocking Options 92

CHAPTER 7 103

Choosing and Placing SPS 103

CHAPTER 8 110

Mounting & Acclimating SPS Frags 110

CHAPTER 9 114

The Benefits of Keeping a Slightly "Dirty" Tank 114

CHAPTER 10 122

Stable Parameters Equals Happy SPS 122

CHAPTER 11 126

AEFW & Red Bugs 126
Prevention 126
Managing Outbreaks 129

CHAPTER 12 132

Problematic Algae 132
A Key to Prevention – Excess Nutrient Control 132
Dealing With an Outbreak 141

CHAPTER 13 152

Husbandry 152

CHAPTER 14 158

Preventing Disasters 158

CHAPTER 15 163

Photography 163
General Tips on Photographing Reef Tanks 163
Tips on Macro Photography For Reef Tanks 172
Progression Shots 179

CHAPTER 16 184

Conclusions – Top 10 Tips 184
References 189

Acknowledgements

This book project took three years to complete and boy it was a lot harder then I ever imagined! For starters, I would like to thank my wife Ginger for putting up with this crazy hobby of mine over the last 25+ years. Thank God she really doesn't know how much I have spent on all the coral, fish and equipment! My daughter Katie also deserves kudos for her interest in my tanks and willingness to accompany me when she was young to local fish stores. Of course I had to bribe her with roast beef sandwiches at the deli but at least I had some company.

So how did this whole obsession begin? My father deserves the most kudos for getting me into the hobby when I was a kid since his fish only saltwater tanks put the aquarium bug in my head. I would also like to recognize Chris Jessen, who was the owner of a local fish store near my former home in Westchester County, New York. The knowledge I picked up from Chris when I started the hobby was invaluable. He was also the one who hooked me on SPS, so I'm not sure if I should thank him or blame him considering the $$$ I spent at his store :)

I would also like to thank Jason Edward, who is the owner of Greenwich Aquaria in Riverside, Connecticut. He was a big help in advising me on setting up my largest SPS tank (225 gallons). Jason really knows his stuff and has one of the most incredible reefs on display in his store.

Online discussion boards such as Reef Central and Reef2Reef have also been great resources for me over the years for gathering information and insights from folks who have had success. And local frag swaps, especially the one put on by Manhattan Reefs, have been invaluable, allowing me to connect with vendors, industry experts and follow hobbyists.

Finally, many thanks to my editor Courtney Jenkins for her professional advice and assistance in polishing this manuscript.

CHAPTER ONE

Introduction

How I Became a ReefBum

WHEN I WAS GROWING up my father kept large saltwater fish tanks. This was back when coral reef tanks were not a viable option for hobbyists. I fondly remember accompanying him to fish stores to check out and purchase fish for his tank. My mom essentially tolerated the hobby, letting my dad do his thing although she would protest about wanting her living room back.

One day my dad had this great idea to go out and buy a ribbon eel. Eels have a reputation as escape artists so my dad did his due diligence and "eel proofed" the tank. Despite my dad's best efforts, that eel found some way to get out of the tank and ended up dead on the living room floor. Of course it was discovered by my poor mom, who nearly jumped through the ceiling. That mischievous eel also traumatized my sister, as it took a few days to find and she was terrified that it would crawl into her bed while it was MIA.

Undeterred, my father tried again with a beautiful chocolate brown Zebra Moray eel. That eel escaped as well and was found on the floor, stiff and covered with dog hair. He plunked it back in the tank and miraculously it survived, living a long and healthy life.

Zebra Moray Eel

Those episodes almost ended my father's fish keeping days, but he assured my mom that all livestock would furthermore remain in the tank. My mom bit her upper lip and let him keep the tank, despite the possibility of more carpet surfing fish in the future. She could see that he had a true passion for keeping salt water tanks, and that passion, or maybe it was an obsession, was passed along to me.

My own first fish tank was a two gallon aquarium I purchased to house an unexpected gold fish. Many years ago my future wife and I visited the San Gennaro festival, New York City's oldest and largest street fair that runs for two weeks in Little Italy, and proceeded to eat, drink and be merry. Amidst said merriment, I was encouraged to play one of those carnival games in which you try to throw a ping pong ball into a gold fish bowl to win a gold fish.

I had no desire to win a gold fish, but I caved to pressure from my future wife to give it a shot. Hey, these games are rigged and nobody ever wins, right? Wrong. I won that gold fish at some ungodly hour that night, and early the next morning I awoke to realize that I now had to go out and find it a suitable home. I didn't know anything about keeping a gold fish, but I found a pet shop that sold me the two gallon tank and some supplies, and gave me advice on what to do. Well, that fish didn't survive too long, but I was hooked.

Next up was a 29 gallon fresh water tank in which I kept live plants, Congo Tetras and other miscellaneous fish. I was intrigued by the beauty of the live plants and how they grew, making the tank look so natural. It felt like creating art, and something inside of me wanted to make more. This was back in the early nineties, and at that point certain advancements in the hobby had made it much easier to keep salt water reef tanks in the home. I was intrigued and, inspired by memories of my father's hobby, I bought a bunch of books to read up on how to keep this type of tank.

I originally ended up buying a 90 gallon reef tank that was broken down when we moved to a new house, where I upgraded to a 120 gallon reef tank. We moved again a number of years later and I went "big" and set up a 225 gallon reef tank.

I have been keeping reef tanks for over twenty-five years now, so it is safe to say that I have developed a love affair with the hobby. It is undeniably in my blood. However, a few years ago I broke down the 225 gallon tank right before Hurricane Sandy hit the New York tri-state area. My family and I had a place in Vermont and during the winter months we would make the pilgrimage up there on weekends, a lot. I had always done my tank maintenance on weekends, so the constant trips away from home began to impact my ability and desire to keep up with the demands of the tank. My corporate job and 4 hour round trip commute to New York City (yes, 4 hours every day!), made it nearly impossible to do my tank chores during the week. So the ski house won out.

It was fortunate timing, since my full-house back-up generator in New York went on the fritz and left me and my family without power for six days. Things do happen for a reason and I truly believe the reef gods were looking over my shoulder and guiding me with divine intervention to take that timely sabbatical.

It felt really strange not to have a tank. The house was dissonantly quiet without the hum of the equipment and the splashing of the tank's turbulent water. Something just seemed off. Predictably, I couldn't keep myself away, as I continued to visit aquarium shops and to lurk on reef tank discussion boards such as Reef Central, Reef2Reef and Manhattan Reefs. Essentially, I knew I would be back.

More recently, events led my wife and I to make Vermont our permanent home, and the ensuing stability in location reignited my desire to get back into the hobby. I "downsized" and set up my latest reef in a 187 gallon tank. Boy, what an adventure I had picking up and moving that aquarium into the house!

CHAPTER 2
Reefology 101

MY MAIN GOAL WITH this book is to relate the insights I've gained with my successes (and failures) in keeping an SPS (small polyp stony coral) dominated reef tank, and how I have achieved optimal growth rates and colors. To do so, I will cover a number of topics including equipment, aquascaping, optimal parameters, husbandry and pest/nuisance algae control, interspersed with a sprinkling of (hopefully;) amusing personal anecdotes. Much of the subject matter will focus on SPS reefs, but there will also be info applying to all types of captive reefs, including a principle I abide by called Reefology.

Is Reefology really a word? Not according to the dictionary, but in my book, both figuratively and literally, it is the science behind the science of reef keeping. Specifically, it refers to practicing the basic principles of doing your homework, being patient, and keeping things simple.

Knowledge is Power

Reef keeping can be an addictive hobby for many, and one culprit that can feed the addiction is the instant gratification reefers seek when scoping out other mature reef tanks. It might be that beautiful 400 gallon display tank one may be eyeballing at a local fish store, or it could be that stunning display being ogled online.

My advice is to not jump in right away and go big in terms of tank size and complexity of the system. It's important to do some due diligence and talk to people who have had success in the hobby, pick their brains and ask to see their setups. Most reef keepers are show offs, myself included, and would welcome the opportunity to do some show and tell. It's also beneficial to read a few books penned by some of the industry experts and to peruse the online discussion boards to gather insights from those who have had success. Read, read, and read some more.

A local frag swap is another great way to become knowledgeable and to meet a lot of like-minded folks. This mosh pit-like scene provides a unique opportunity to do some reef keeping speed dating and connect with tons of vendors and fellow hobbyists.

Some Nice Eye Candy For Sale at a Swap

Many swaps also bring in industry experts who do lectures on topics that are beneficial to both beginners and experts. I have attended many swaps, and they are fantastic troves of info. The key is to become a sponge and to soak up as much gleanable knowledge as possible. Homework is not just a requirement for newbies. Veterans also have to be diligent when trying something new.

I learned this the hard way, and made a mistake that sent one of my former tanks into a tailspin, causing it to crash. It was years ago and at the time there were these new double-ended HQI metal halide bulbs getting rave reviews for their ability to grow and color up corals. My SPS were doing just ok so I figured it would be worth it to try something new. I used the lights for a while and didn't achieve the desired results, so I was on the hunt for another solution. The guy at my local fish store had a kick ass SPS tank lit by standard mogul metal halide bulbs, only he didn't have any glass lenses/shields between them and the tank. He felt the glass decreased the PAR (Photosynthetically Available Radiation, which is all radiation between 400-700 nm wavelength range) on the lights, so he removed the glass despite the risk of water splashing on the bulbs and cracking them. Hmm, removing the glass lenses, now maybe that's the ticket!

Unfortunately, the double-ended HQI bulbs did not have the UV protected glass present on the mogul style bulbs. The UV protection was built into the glass lenses in the fixture, and when I removed them I fried pretty much everything in the tank. All of my SPS died within a matter of hours and I lost most of my fish, a testament to the severity of the damaging UV rays emanating from the bulbs. I didn't do my homework and I paid the price.

Patience is a Virtue

Patience is another important key to success, and it's vital to not lose it in the quest for instant gratification. A good way to get your feet wet in this hobby (pardon the pun) is to start with a FOWLR (fish only with live rock) tank. This is a great way to ease into things and develop an understanding of what it takes to keep a reef. Adding in some hardy soft corals such as mushrooms, zooanthids or leather corals is the next step once success is achieved with a FOWLR tank.

Zooanthids

It really helps to be systematic and to not get in over one's head. Mistakes will be made, and corals and fish will be lost. It happens to EVERYBODY. However, the losses can be minimized if lessons are learned from those mistakes, so it's critical to be patient and do the required homework.

Keeping more demanding hard corals such as SPS is next in the progression and it will require some equipment upgrades (lighting, calcium supplementation, etc). Again, I would suggest starting with some of the more hardy corals such as branching or cupping Montipora. In a different vein, patience is also crucial on a daily basis while maintaining a tank.

Orange Montipora

Resist The Urge to Submerge

One practice for reef keeping that I adhere to is minimizing the amount of time I put my hands in the tank. I consider myself a perfectionist and when I started to keep reefs I was always looking at my tanks and tinkering with the rocks or corals to achieve a "better" look.

I would buy a new coral and spend a lot of time trying to place it just right, moving it from spot to spot. This stressed out the coral and made it tough for it to establish itself in its new environment. What I learned over time is that Mother Nature needs to be let alone to do her thing.

It's best to put the coral in a spot and just let it be. Well, what if a frag tips over? Not to worry. I have seen some hobbyists intentionally glue a frag horizontally to a frag plug to allow multiple branches to spring up vertically. A healthy frag or coral will find its way when left alone. The constant touching will not only cause stress, it will introduce oils from a person's skin which may upset the delicate balance of the tank.

Properly aquascaping a tank with rock when initially setting up a reef is very important, since it will really help to minimize the amount of time one has to fuss with corals down the road. The key is to create a stable structure that looks natural and has lots of shelves on which to place future corals. An avalanche of rocks is the last thing a reefer wants to occur after a reef matures. If you need to get those hands wet over and over again while achieving your desired effect, then it is best to do it at the beginning to make sure a solid foundation is achieved. The negative side effects will be minimal since the reef is still very young.

Build a Solid & Natural Looking Aquascape

Finally, patience also comes into play with young reef tanks, especially those started with just frags. This stage can feel unsatisfying because a young tank looks sparse with a lot of open real estate, but have faith. Once an adequate number of corals are added, a reef keeper should essentially sit back and watch. Corals will grow in a healthy tank, so it is very important to anticipate growth and to be sure to give them room to expand. Constantly adding new corals to "fill in the blank spots" will cause problems down the road, as it will restrict flow, a key ingredient to SPS health.

I get into greater detail on both aquascaping and coral placement in subsequent chapters but the main lessons here are to keep the tinkering to a minimum and to give corals time to grow.

The KISS Principle of Reef Keeping

Reef keepers today have many varying options available to run a reef tank, with different methods that require certain pieces of equipment and specific supplements and additives. There is no right or wrong way, and folks have had success with many different types of setups.

The myriad choices can be daunting and sometimes folks end up chasing their own tails by trying different things, in piece meal or in a vacuum, employed by others who have achieved success. The thinking goes something like this: "That guy doses amino acids and has great colors with his SPS so that must be the ticket." When that doesn't work they add something else to the mix by, for instance, trying a different supplement. Or maybe the experiment is equipment related. Sometimes changes are made on an impromptu basis, a risky proposition considering the delicate nature of captive reef aquaria.

Stability is crucial to the success of reef keeping, so constant change is not good.

Simplicity is important as well. Over the years, I have found it more prudent to have fewer moving parts when it comes to keeping a reef tank. According to Wikipedia, the "KISS" principle (Keep It Simple, Stupid) states that most systems work best if they are kept simple rather than made overly complicated, so simplicity should be a key goal in your design and unnecessary complexity should be avoided.

My advice is to stick to this principle and avoid turning a tank into a science experiment with a whole bunch of components/pieces of equipment. The chances of something going wrong are greater when more variables are in play, so less is more. The same is true when it comes to additives and supplements. Having a complicated dosing regime can be risky if you are not in touch with how certain supplements impact others. Overdosing then becomes a risk.

In my experience, I have achieved success when I kept things simple and followed the other basic principles of Reefology. Nothing good ever happened when I was constantly searching for that magic bullet.

CHAPTER 3

Equipment & Filtration

Choosing The Right Aquarium

AQUARIUM MANUFACTURERS offer a ton of options on standard aquariums that satisfy the needs of many reef keepers. My first reef tank was a standard acrylic tank and it served me well for years. Eventually, as I gained experience, I discovered that I wanted certain features in a tank that were not standard options, so I went the custom route.

Custom aquariums are typically more expensive then standard tanks but the extra expense should be viewed as an investment that will provide you with years of enjoyment. It is important to do a lot of research and to talk with a number of custom tank manufacturers, getting at least three cost quotes. It is also worthwhile to ask other hobbyists about their experiences with manufactures. This will increase the odds of finding a company willing to stand behind its product with good customer service.

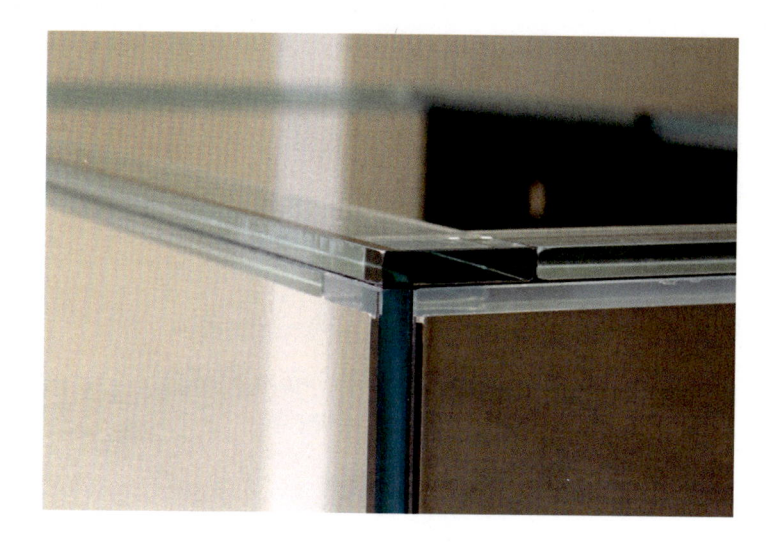

In terms of tank size, I recommend not biting off more then one can chew, as it is important to have the means and bandwidth to take on the expense and maintenance of a large tank. On the plus side, a big tank will be a more stable ecosystem since parameters such as temperature, pH, and alkalinity will not swing as much as they would in a smaller tank.

Once tank size is determined there are a few different options to consider regarding the tank's dimensions. It's important to think ahead about the rock and coral placement and growth. I always like to go as wide as possible since the added depth provides some cool aquascaping options. A wider tank can also improve flow and help prevent dead spots in the tank.

External overflows can also be beneficial when it comes to flow since they do not protrude into the tank, as is the case with internal overflows, which can create funky 'dead' spots. External overflows also provide a cleaner look and make it easier to keep the back panel of the tank clean. I think this is critical since a clean back panel makes it easier for corals and fish to stand out or "pop" visually.

External Overflow

Going with an open top tank that is rimless or eurobraced will also provide a clean look and open up more viewing angles. I like to think of open top tanks as four dimensional, with viewing through the front, both sides and top.

Another option I highly recommend with a custom tank is low iron glass. The clarity is much better then standard glass and is well worth the upgrade. Low iron glass is a bit more prone to scratches then regular glass so one does have to be careful.

The Clean and Sleek Look of an Open Top Tank

Acrylic is used by many who opt for large tanks since the material is much lighter than glass. It also has great clarity but is much more prone to scratches, although these can be removed with some work.

With regards to tank plumbing, I do not like to have any drains or return lines far below the water line. Some do this with external re-circulating pumps to create flow in hard to reach spots near the bottom of the tank, but I think it is just too risky given the chance a bulkhead leaks or fails. Enough flow can easily be created by using internal re-circulating pumps such as the Ecotech MP40.

As you can see, there are a lot of options available to customize a "dream" tank. If the custom route is taken, allow for extra time for the tank to be built. Some manufactures take longer then others, so I recommend getting an estimate in writing. Anything longer then an 8-10 week turnaround for a custom tank without a lot of bells and whistles could be a red flag, as the manufacturer might be exceeding its capacity to build tanks and meet deadlines.

Here are the specifications for my current tank:

- 60"L x 30"D x 24"H, 187g Euro-Braced Glass Aquarium
- Starphire Low-Iron Glass Front & 2 End Panels and Painted Black Background
- 21"L External Overflow Box
- 36"H Traditional Style Stand w/Raised-Panel Doors, Fluted Trim Moldings and Water-Resistant Pan Liner

187 Gallon Tank & Stand

Lesson #1 via Amusing Personal Anecdote

The time of year matters when purchasing a custom aquarium, especially in areas that get snow or, as we generally hope for in Vermont, a Lot of snow.

My Epic Journey Begins

Winters in my home state of Vermont can be harsh and unpredictable. I knew this when I contemplated ordering my tank during December, so I had a dilemma: go for it and receive the tank during the middle of March, when winter still lingers, or wait until much warmer weather arrives in the middle of May. I would have to wait the additional two months due to "mud season," considered our fifth season here in Vermont (mud season usually begins at the end of March and lasts a few weeks, although it can begin later and stretch to the end of April). During mud season the dirt road I live on turns into a soupy, sloppy, mess. At times it can be barely passable for an SUV, so a truck delivering the tank would never make it.

Given my desire to get the tank up and running, I decided to roll the dice and have it delivered in mid-March. The tank builder was very accommodating when it came to scheduling a pick up date, and that was critical due to the volatility of the weather. The manufacturer was right on schedule with the build, so about ten days before the due date I began to monitor the weather. Long-term forecasts were calling for dry and mild weather beginning the third week of March so I decided to tentatively schedule pick-up during the first part of that week. Very cold weather is not good for the tank's silicon so temperature was also a big factor in fine tuning a pick up date.

I rented a sixteen-foot box truck and honed in on the Monday of that week as the pick-up date. It is a six hour drive from my house to the tank builder's location in New Jersey so my plan was to pick the tank up that Monday, sleep at a friend's house that night and then head up to Vermont early the next morning. A moving crew was lined up for that afternoon to help move the tank from the truck to its final resting spot in my walkout basement.

The trip down went well and it was great to finally see the tank and stand.

The tank and stand were loaded onto the truck in the afternoon and I headed to my friend's house in Connecticut to rest up for the last leg of my return trip.

I awoke about 4:15 the next morning and immediately checked the weather radar for Vermont. The forecast had been getting progressively worse for move-in day, so I was a bit anxious to say the least. Upon consulting the radar my worst fears were realized. A large blob of rain, freezing rain and snow were making their way across New York and into Vermont. Oh boy. Fortunately, it was just raining when I left my friend's house in Connecticut, but the wiper blades on the truck were shot, making for some white knuckle driving in the dark during the first part of the trip.

Once it became light out, I stopped and checked the radar. Good news, it looked like the blob was going to be past Vermont by the time I arrived. Phew! I continued on my way and, as predicted, the weather started to clear. But then it changed. About an hour south of my house I noticed some dark, ominous clouds ahead. I didn't even want to check the radar. This being Vermont, the weather can change on a dime.

It was starting to sleet when I finally made it to the first of two dirt roads leading to my house. Instantly my heart started to pound a bit wondering whether the truck would make it over the hard snow and ice that had formed on the road. The tires on this truck were not bald, but I didn't have a lot of confidence in their ability to navigate this wintery mix.

I made it past the first road just fine and then slowly meandered down my road to our driveway. Our driveway is not long, but it has a very small descent, yet I thought I would be fine even if it was a little icy. Well, it was quite icy and as I crept down the small slope at a snail's pace the truck's wheels started to slide. It skated a few feet and stopped. I drove tentatively for another foot or so, slid a bit more, and managed somehow to bring her to a stop. I tried this again, and the truck started to skid to the right and veer towards the trees on the side of the driveway. My heart was racing at this point and all I could envision, after my 800 mile journey, was the truck stuck in the ditch near the top of our driveway, making it impossible to safely offload the precious cargo.

Somehow, with white knuckles and held breath, I was able to right the truck and get it pointed straight down the driveway again. About halfway down, I managed to put it in park and applied the emergency brake, in order to get out and find something with which to improve the traction. As I took a step toward the garage to fetch some boards, I turned to see the truck sliding down the driveway without me!!! Oh sh$$%t!! Miraculously it stopped of its own accord and, jumping back behind the wheel, I was able then to safely drive it down the rest of the way.

The sleet had become thicker and had started to turn to snow, covering the 100 foot path I had cleared through the backyard to the walkout basement. As the snow became heavier, this path of grass, dirt and broad slate steps was beginning to get dangerously slick, and I was wondering whether I should cancel the movers who were due to arrive in an hour. The problem with postponing the movers was that temperatures were predicted to plummet that afternoon, so keeping the tank in the truck or in my unheated garage would be very risky given what I mentioned before about silicon not doing well in the cold.

I decided to wait for the movers to arrive and get their assessment of the situation. One of the guys in charge rolled in and promptly told me they could not be held responsible for any damage given the current weather. It was puking snow at this point but they were willing to give it a go, so I kept my fingers tightly crossed.

My Icy Driveway

The stand made it in just fine and next up was the tank. We made a large dolly for it to sit on and laid down a bunch of plywood on the path to the basement for the dolly to roll on. It worked great and the only hitch was when the guys had to carry the tank and dolly over the two different sets of slick slate stairs. When the tank made it inside I was overwhelmed with relief. What a memorable journey, one that I won't forget for the rest of my life. Note to self: order the next tank during the summer!!

Sumps

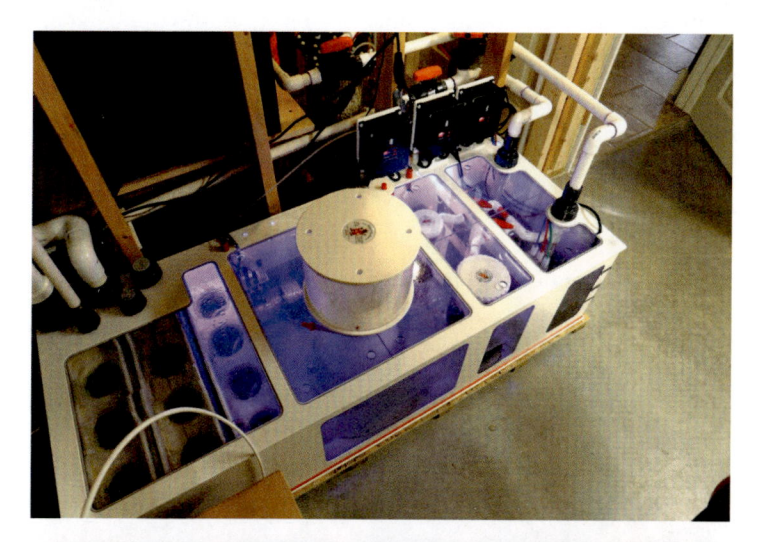

Custom Sump

There are many choices out there for sumps, including standard cookie cutter sumps designed to work with a variety of different setups. The flexibility is a bonus since one is not locked into a specific configuration and can more easily swap out equipment housed in this type of sump, such as a return pump or skimmer.

A custom sump is a more expensive option but they are designed to work together with the equipment inside the sump, making them easier to operate and maintain. These units are typically more self-contained with lids to limit evaporation. I have a custom sump for my 187 gallon tank and I can certainly say the benefits justify the extra expense.

Remote Sumps

Sump Located in a Remote Location

Having enough space for all of the equipment necessary to run a thriving reef tank is an issue faced by most reef keepers. A custom sump will help on this front but it is not always the answer. Sometimes it is necessary to go with a remote sump.

Besides requiring more room for equipment, there are a few other reasons why it may make sense to have a remote area for a sump and the rest of the equipment:

- Less risk of water splashing on and damaging electrical plugs and equipment.
- Fewer heat sources underneath the tank (equipment such as pumps and light ballasts do generate heat).
- Less noise in the living area where the tank is located.
- Less water underneath the tank, making water damage less likely for a wooden stand.
- Less hassle when doing tank maintenance.

One potential solution, before taking the step to locate equipment away from the tank, is to expand the current space around the tank. In my first house my tank was in a finished basement against a wall with all of the equipment below the stand. We had plans to renovate the basement so that gave me an opportunity to be creative and do a better job integrating the tank into the living space. It also gave me an excuse to get a bigger tank!

A contractor cut a hole in the wall for the new tank, and he also created a "closet" behind the tank for all of the equipment. This gave me much more room and it also allowed me to hide the equipment. It was a big improvement from my prior setup but I still had to keep some equipment, such as my RO/DI (reverse osmosis and deionization) water purification unit and reservoir in a separate location.

What choices exist for a remote sump? A great way to go, if feasible, is to have a remote sump in a basement below the tank. When I lived in Connecticut my tank was located in our living room and I had my equipment underneath, in the unfinished basement. Gravity allowed the water to drain downstairs and I simply pumped water back upstairs to complete the cycle. I used two return pumps to give me additional output for a frag tank downstairs and more power to circulate water in the display tank. It also provided me with some redundancy in case one of my pumps failed.

Plumbing with PVC through the floor to the basement was not easy, so a decent amount of skill in this area is required. Reinforced flexible tubing is also an option, although it is not as sturdy as PVC. If plumbing skills are lacking, another avenue is to seek out a reefing buddy who can help.

Plumbing in Basement Underneath Display Tank

As for expense, it will cost more for this type of two-story setup since more pumping power is required to move water upstairs. However, a big benefit to having all of the equipment in a basement is natural temperature moderation. Typically, basements below ground-level are much cooler than a house in the summer and warmer in the winter, so both the chiller and heater do not have to work as hard, resulting in lower electricity bills. Another option for a remote sump is to locate it in an adjacent room on the same level as the tank. For my 187 gallon setup the equipment is in a workroom next to the room housing the tank. I simply drilled some holes in the wall between the two rooms to accommodate the plumbing, with two holes for drain lines and two holes for return lines. Aesthetically, my preference was to drill holes in the wall behind the tank but that was not possible. My plan was to cover up the pipes, but the "industrial" look grew on me, so I left them out in the open.

PVC Pipe Through Wall to Remote Sump

Grey PVC Pipe Blending In

The trick to using an adjacent room is to make sure the sump is lower than the tank in order for gravity to do its job. The farther away the tank, the harder it becomes to employ this method. My sump is about 15 feet away from the tank and the top is about 16 inches from the ground. The bottom of my external overflow is 52 inches from the ground, so I had about three feet to play with to plumb down to the sump.

A garage is another potential place to locate a sump but that is limited to warm weather climates. Ultimately, a remote sump is a great way to go if you can swing it.

Connecting the Tank to the Sump: Designing a Plumbing Roadmap

When starting a reef tank, it is always a great idea to lay out plans for how all of the equipment will be plumbed together and connected to the tank. I call it a plumbing roadmap. I start by breaking out a pad of paper and doodling some sketches to see what works and what doesn't work. Once I am happy with my design, I bring it to life on the computer with some more defined and legible sketches (my handwriting is the worst).

Sketchup is a great program for this purpose and I highly recommend it for anybody who has the skill set to work with this type of software. I am not a Sketchup expert so when I set out to draw the design for my 187 gallon tank I leaned mostly on PowerPoint with a little help from Sketchup.

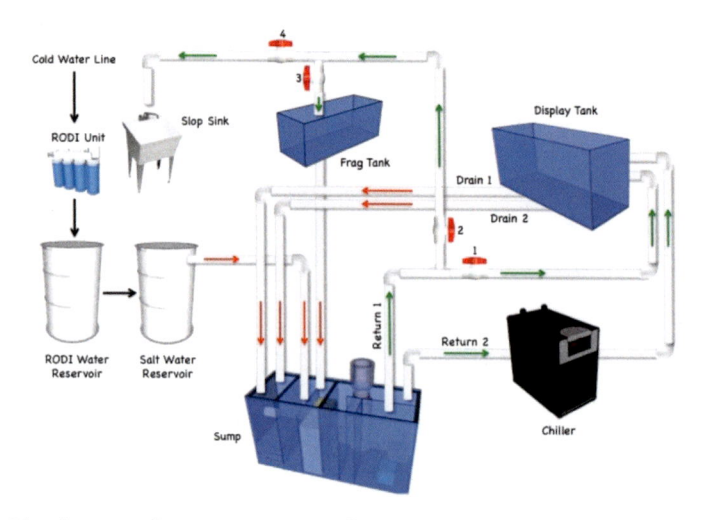

Plumbing Roadmap For My 187 Gallon Reef Tank

As for the specifics of my design, my goal was to come up with an efficient way to plumb together my sump, display tank and frag tank, and to also have the ability to easily do large water changes. I really like having two return pumps in case one fails, and this extra pump serves a vital role in my design.

Return Pump 1 was set up to send water from the sump to both the display tank and the frag tank while Return Pump 2 also fed water from the sump through the chiller, then to the display tank. Additionally, Return Pump 2 would be utilized to feed water through a media reactor in the sump containing carbon (not shown in the diagram). Ball valves 1, 2 and 3 would be open while 4 would be closed.

To do water changes, I do the following:

- Shut the system down
- Close ball valves 1 & 3
- Open ball valve 4
- Turn on Return Pump 1
- Drain desired amount of water into slop sink
- Pump an equal amount of water back into the sump from the saltwater reservoir
- Open ball valves 1 & 3 (2 is already open) and close 4
- Restart system

After a water change, I utilize a pump in my RO/DI reservoir to pump RO/DI water into the salt water reservoir, mix it with salt and heat it to the desired temperature, giving me a new batch of water for the next water change.

This might seem to be a complicated setup but my goal was to keep it as simple as possible (the KISS principle) while making the tank easier to run and maintain. In the long run, the time I spent thinking it through paid off.

Lesson #2 via Amusing Personal Anecdote: A Leak!

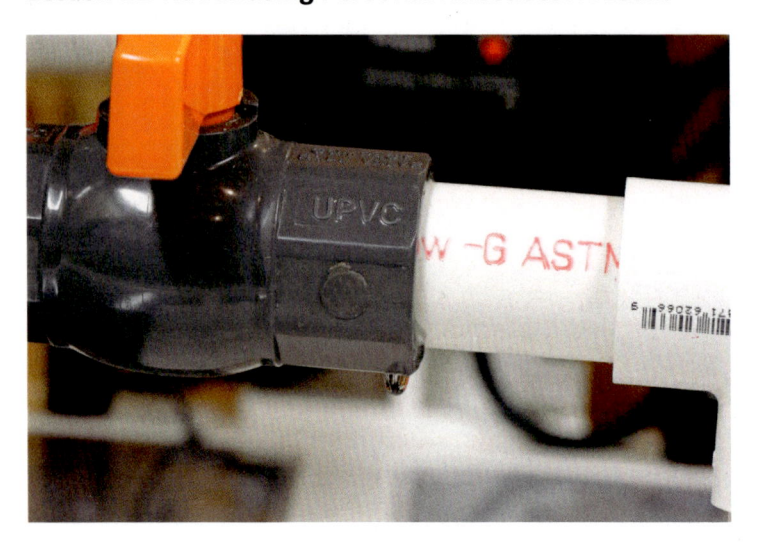

And another leak. And another one. Oh boy. I had just spent four days plumbing my new tank to the filtration system and when I fired up the pumps for the first time I had more leaks then I could count. This 187 gallon build was going to test my patience.

Over the years I had become quite proficient at using PVC to build my tank systems, so having such a large scale failure with my latest venture was a surprise. How did it happen? The main culprit was tied to a habit that drives my wife crazy, my obsession to be neat.

I don't like mess, and things can get pretty sloppy when using PVC primer and glue. When I put my last tank together eight years ago I got purple PVC primer all over the white PVC used for the sump and other filtration equipment, which was out of sight in my unfinished basement. There were no major leaks but it looked very sloppy.

This time I was bent on having a more clean and polished look for my new filtration system even though it too would be in a remote location away from the display tank. I had two ideas to achieve my goal: use clear PVC primer instead of purple and go lighter on the glue. Heck, I never had any major leaks before so I probably used way more glue in my last build then necessary. Wrong.

Let's start with the primer. If you are going to use clear primer then you better have a system in place to make sure you actually applied it and the glue to where it is supposed to go. In many towns it is against code for plumbers to use clear primer since there is no visual evidence for inspectors to see if fittings were primed and glued. Residential aquariums are not normally inspected, so clear primer is fair game, but it really helps to set up some sort of verification system.

Clear primer was responsible for one of my leaks when I thought one fitting was glued but it wasn't. From that point forward I used a Sharpie and put a little "G" (for glue) as a reminder on each fitting after it was primed and glued. I would also recommend doing this if purple primer is used on grey schedule 80 PVC, since it is hard to see purple on this type of PVC.

Ultimately, the majority of my leaks were tied to going too light on the glue. I had glued the sockets of fittings but not the pipes. The neat freak inside of me assumed it would be ok to apply liberal amounts of glue to just the sockets, a rookie mistake indeed.

The leaks that appeared right away were in the pressurized return lines. Some were pretty big and others were barely perceptible. I knew what I had to do; redo all of my return lines. Ugh, countless hours of hard work down the drain and more hours on tap (pardon my plumbing puns!) to re-plumb everything.

Well, it took two days to redo everything and when I was done I fired the system back up, confident I had solved the problem. 24 hours later I had no leaks in the return lines but I started to notice leaks in the drain lines. I had assumed that I didn't need to re-glue the drain lines since they weren't pressurized. Wrong again.

It took another two days to tear down and rebuild all of the drain lines. Did I think about just fixing the fittings that were leaking? Yes, but I opted to do everything since I wanted to make sure this wouldn't be an issue down the road.

What did I learn from all of this? It doesn't always pay to be neat! Actually, I found out the hard way how careful you need to be when using clear PVC primer and why it is a bad

*idea to skimp on glue. My experience also reminded me how important it is to fix
even very slow leaks, given how they can get bigger over time.*

Overall, it helps to be patient (that word again!), when plumbing a tank, because it can be a complicated task. My advice is to not freak out when a trace of water suddenly appears on the floor or a fitting. Everything is fixable and it is better to put the time in to rectify a problem when building a system versus dealing with it when the reef is mature.

Lighting: My Success With Metal Halides

In my years of experience in keeping SPS dominated reef tanks, I have had a lot of success using metal halides with supplemental T5 lighting. Specifically, my SPS have achieved great color and growth with 400W, 20000K Radiums, which skew towards the blue end of the spectrum. Some reefers use only T5s and have awesome looking tanks while others have done really well with LEDs.

The technology for LED lighting has come a long way and has gained popularity among many who have used T5s and metal halides. LED lights can be pricier but they run cooler than halides (therefore it is less likely you'll need a chiller) and typically use less electricity. LED bulbs also have a very long life span vs. metal halide and T5 bulbs, so extra money will be saved on replacing bulbs down the line. Additionally, high output LED lights now have enough PAR to grow SPS that demand a lot of light.

LED lighting also has less spillage, with more of the light focused on corals versus the back or sides of the tank, although metal halide and T5 users point to this as a disadvantage given the better light spread produced by reflectors in those light fixtures. Furthermore, LED lights are dimmable, making it easy to adjust the output of LEDs to reproduce different types of lighting conditions such as a bright or a cloudy day. Also, you have the ability to easily change the color spectrum, giving reef keepers many different options to play with.

Despite how far LED lighting has come over the last few years, I decided based on personal experience to stick with a combination of metal halides and T5s for my latest SPS dominated tank, which I started in 2015.

My 225 Gallon Tank Under Metal Halides and T5s

Would I use LEDs today? Perhaps, given some of the stunning tanks I have seen online and in person lit by the EcoTech Marine Radion LED light fixtures.

Calcium and Alkalinity Supplementation

A reef tank dominated with SPS can be a bit like a teenage boy. It has a big appetite and can quickly eat you out of house and home. Similar to how boys can consume large quantities of Ring Dings and Yodels (ok, I'm showing my age here), SPS can suck up a lot of calcium and alkalinity. These corals have calcium skeletons and demand a lot of calcium and alkalinity supplementation to grow and thrive within an aquarium.

The relationship between calcium and alkalinity is a complex one and I will defer to the chemistry experts to explain the dynamics between the two. What I would like to address here are the different options available for calcium and alkalinity supplementation.

When I started to keep reef tanks, I kept mostly soft corals and began to experiment with SPS only after achieving success with them. I used a two part calcium and alkalinity supplement from ESV and it worked great. As I added more SPS, my calcium and alkalinity demands grew, requiring more of the two-part solution. Cost can be a downside when using certain two-part solutions for tanks requiring a lot of calcium and alkalinity supplementation, but some SPS enthusiasts swear by it, since it is a ready made and simple to use solution. You will need to calculate the amounts needed and add them (manually or via some automated doser) on a daily basis.

Another way to supplement calcium and alkalinity is to use a kalk reactor. Kalkwasser is used in conjunction with RO/DI water that is either gravity fed or forced through the unit via a separate dosing pump. The kalkwasser and RO/DI water need to be mixed, and a unit such as the one sold by My Reef Creations uses a pump attached to the reactor to do the mixing.

My Reef Creations Kalk Reactor

Kalk reactors are great but they do struggle on their own to keep up when calcium and alkalinity demands are high. You get the most bang for your buck with a calcium reactor, and the one sold by Marine Technical Concepts is great for systems that require a lot of calcium and alkalinity. Once dialed in, these units allow you to "set it and forget it".

Marine Technical Concepts PROCAL Calcium Reactor

The pH of the effluent coming out of a calcium reactor is low, so sometimes it is necessary to also use a kalk reactor to boost pH and further augment calcium and alkalinity. I have had a lot of success using both calcium and kalk reactors with my tanks, although I have also achieved great results using the two-part method I am currently using for my 187 gallon tank.

No matter which path is taken, it is critical to be diligent in testing calcium and alkalinity levels on a regular basis. Calcium in reef aquariums should be kept between 380-450 ppm while alkalinity should be in the 7-11 dKH range.[1] Alkalinity is more important, so I recommend keeping a keen eye on it to keep it stable in order to avoid any large swings and subsequent fading or burnt tips on SPS (my tanks do well between 8-9 dKH).

Success will be achieved when a reefer finds that happy zone and replenishes what the corals consume. Their appetite can be large, so it is important to satisfy the demand.

Go With The Flow: Why Strong Circulation is Important for SPS

Blue Tort

A key factor to keeping a thriving SPS dominated reef tank is having a lot of water movement via strong circulation, and there are a number of reasons why. Number one is to avoid 'dead' spots and to keep detritus (dead organic matter such as fragments of dead organisms or fish waste) from collecting at the bottom, which helps to keep nitrates and phosphates from building up in the tank. Accumulation of these elements can lead to algae outbreaks.

Strong flow also helps to deliver food and nutrients to the corals. Besides strong flow, random flow is also beneficial and can be achieved by hooking pumps up to a controller with preset randomized programs (random flow replicates waves moving across a natural reef).

I am also a believer in having strong surface agitation since it helps to increase oxygen levels and imitates the light refraction in our natural reefs.

Surface Agitation at Top of Tank. Rimless reefs are very popular but I prefer euro-bracing since it prevents water spillage in tanks with strong surface flow.

So what is the right amount of flow to have in an SPS dominated tank? Opinions vary on this but I would recommend a flow rate in the range of 40-60 gallons per hour (GPH). This is the number of times per hour that the water volume in the display tank is moved. As an example, a 200 gallon tank with a GPH of 10,000 would have a flow rate of 50X.[2]

To maximize flow, I recommend being judicious with pump placement inside the tank and having an open rock structure. I'll talk more on this in the aquascaping chapter.

Skimmers

Having an effective protein skimmer is vitally important to maintaining a healthy and thriving SPS dominated reef tank. Skimmers remove organic matter such as fish waste, uneaten food, dying or decaying animals, and problematic algae and bacteria. How do they work? Essentially, a pump pushes water into the column of a skimmer while air is injected, creating a foam. Waste adheres to the air bubbles in the foam and is removed when the foam rises to the top and spills into the collection cup.

There are several types of skimmers one can use. The original type of skimmer available to aquarists was an air driven counter-current skimmer. These skimmers relied on wooden air diffusers and a high capacity pump to generate bubbles. I used to own one and it did require a lot of maintenance and constant water height adjustments to get it dialed in.

A downdraft skimmer, another early design, is typically tall and bulky and needs a strong pump to create air bubbles. Water is sprayed at a high speed into a column that has bio balls. The resulting bubbles flow through the bio balls and then travel into a box where they are pushed up and collected in the neck of the skimmer. Cleaning is not an easy task with this model either, and they are expensive to operate due to the strong pump.

A third type of skimmer is a venturi skimmer, which uses a venturi injector or valve to create air bubbles by drawing air into a water stream. For my 225 gallon tank I used a venturi style skimmer with a Beckett injector, a type of venturi valve. My skimmer had two Beckett injectors and was 50″ tall, a beast to say the least! The Beckett injectors use more air and create a tremendous amount of foam, generating much more power versus other venturi injectors. This skimmer did a great job for me and was very reliable, but the injectors were prone to clogging and had to be cleaned out on a regular basis. On the plus side, this type of skimmer relies on an external pump and does not require a lot of "tuning" to adjust the water level in the skimmer's chamber.

An aspirating skimmer is perhaps the most popular form of skimmer in use today. I use one on my 187 gallon tank and it does a fantastic job. With this skimmer, air is injected into the impeller cavity of a pump to create bubbles, which are chopped up into finer bubbles by an impeller, needle wheel, or pegged wheel. These skimmers are compact and can easily fit inside a sump or underneath a tank stand. They are also easy to set up and maintain. Additionally, they rely on slower water flow and are less expensive to operate since they use low power pumps.[3]

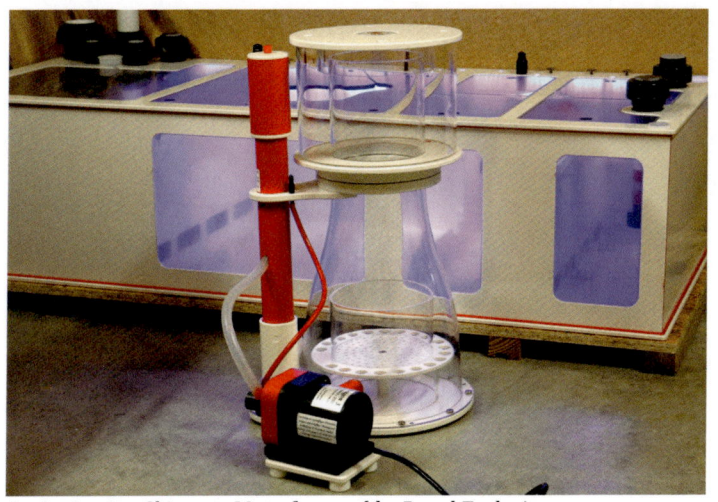

An Aspirating Skimmer Manufactured by Royal Exclusiv

On the downside, there are some durability concerns with certain needle wheel impellers. Some of these units can be tough to dial in, requiring frequent water height adjustments in the chamber when water levels change in the sump.

All skimmers need to be cleaned and maintained on a regular basis to be effective. For basic maintenance on my aspirating skimmer, I clean out my collection cup and upper part of the neck with paper towels once a week.

Skimmer Collection Cup

Self cleaning heads that sit on top of the collection cup and automatically wipe the inside of the cup on a periodic basis are available to make this cleaning process easier. I have heard claims of some heads being able to improve a skimmer's efficiency by up to 30%.

Another accessory to consider is some sort of mechanism to prevent skimmate from suddenly overflowing out of the cup and into the tank or sump. Disaster can strike if this happens and some folks use waste collection containers connected to the skimmer cup to catch the overflow. Some containers, when full, will not prevent waste from continuing to overflow onto the floor, but other devices will shut a skimmer off when the container is full. These automatic shut off containers can be pricey but there are cheaper options.

For my latest skimmer I installed a $10 float switch in my collection cup to shut down the skimmer when skimmate fills the cup. My Neptune Systems Apex Controller is alerted when the switch is triggered and automatically shuts off the skimmer.

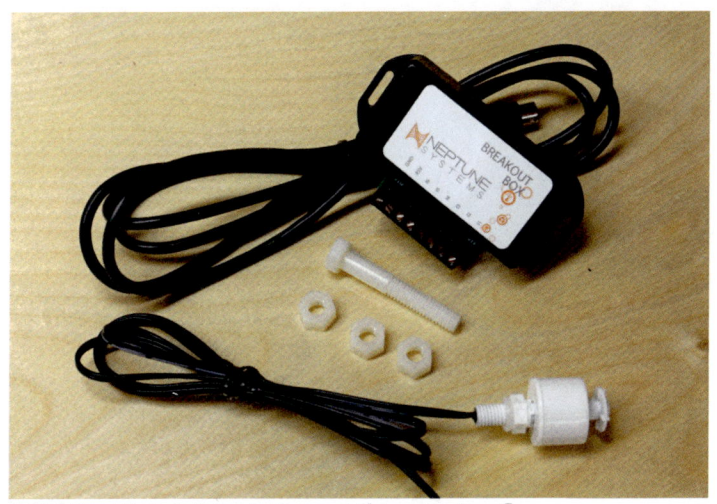

A DIY Float Switch Setup to Prevent Skimming Overflows

In a nutshell, my best advice when it comes to selecting a skimmer is to select a high quality one that is very efficient. It has been a big part of my success with SPS.

Don't assume bigger is better. A skimmer will not be as effective if you use one rated for a large tank on a small tank. Why is this the case? Well, to perform optimally, a skimmer should be working all the time. An oversized skimmer will tend to skim well for a few days then slow down once all of the organics have been skimmed out. Once the organics build up again the skimmer will spring back into action, and thus perform inconsistently.

A UV Sterilizer For a Reef Tank?

Reef keepers have long debated whether the constant use of a UV Sterilizer is helpful or harmful to a saltwater reef tank. In essence, a UV sterilizer has a UV bulb in a watertight compartment that will kill or zap undesirables in the water that pass through the unit. Undesirables include free-floating algae spores, parasites and troublesome bacteria such as heterotrophic bacteria.

A UV will not kill "good guy" beneficial nitrifying bacteria that reside in the sand bed and live rock, and are not free-floating. However, the key question is whether the sterilizer will also kill free-floating microorganisms that are beneficial to corals? Are the benefits worth the risk?[4]

Before I delve into that question, let's take a closer look at the reasons why one would use a UV sterilizer on a constant basis. UV can reduce the amount of parasites in the water column, making it easier to treat an outbreak and reduce the impact of fish disease. However, it won't prevent or eliminate disease. Remember, a UV will kill free-floating microorganisms, but not all of your tank's potential microorganisms are free floating at all stages of life.

Ok, how about using one to maintain crystal clear water? A UV will certainly help in this regard if the water has a green tint, as it does kill free-floating algae spores. However, a UV will not wipe out something like hair algae attached to rocks or corals, it has to be free-floating.[5]

I endorse using means other than using a sterilizer 24/7 to achieve the same dividends. To prevent fish disease, the best course of action is to initially quarantine all new arrivals in a separate tank. As for water clarity, I am a proponent of using activated carbon to keep things crystal clear.

I do believe UV sterilizers are useful in small doses to rectify a problem such as a bacterial bloom, which can occur when too many fish are added to a new aquarium. In this instance, the "good guy" nitrifying bacteria are not fully established and unable to break down all organic waste. The troublesome or "bad" heterotrophic bacteria will act as scavengers and feed off of the organic waste, multiplying rapidly and creating the bloom.[6]

When blooms occur, the bacteria consume a lot of oxygen, so it is important to keep the water oxygenated.[7] One way to do this it to increase flow near the top of the tank, which will increase surface agitation and cause the rate of gas exchange between the water and the air to increase. Higher flow will also help to suspend detritus and improve exportation of the organic matter that can feed a bloom.

Does it make sense to do a series of large water changes before trying a UV sterilizer? Probably not, because the "bad" bacteria can reproduce very quickly.[8] I didn't see any improvement after I tried this. However, cleaning the filter socks more frequently, vacuuming the gravel to remove detritus and not overfeeding the fish should help.

It is very important to figure out the source of a problem so it can be avoided in the future. Without this knowledge a reefer is only putting a band-aid on the problem.

Before use of UV Sterilizer

2 Days After Use of UV Sterilizer

Filtration

There are three main types of filtration for a reef tank: biological, mechanical and chemical.

Biological filtration converts waste products produced by organisms in the tank to a non-toxic state. Live rock and sand are great hangouts for these bacteria, which will break down ammonia and nitrite into nitrogen compounds that are safer for the reef's inhabitants.

Mechanical filtration is the process of removing undissolved particles from the water, eliminating organic matter before it has a chance to break down. This can be accomplished with the use of filter pads, pre-filter sponges or filter socks (the method I use).

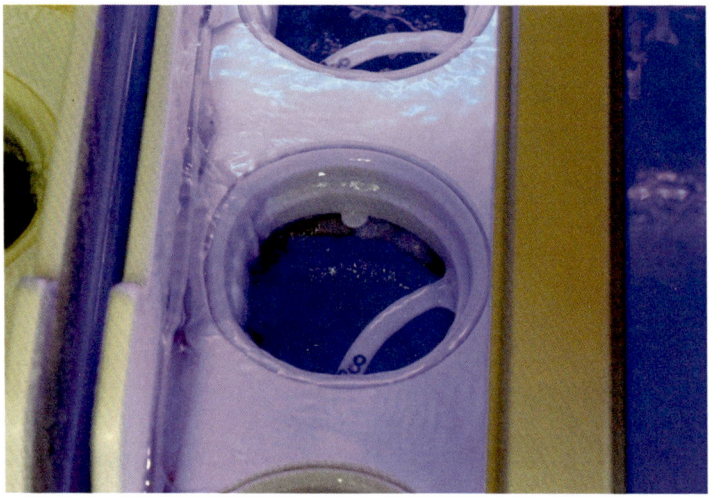

Filter Socks

Finally, chemical filtration is used to remove dissolved organic compounds that can give water a yellow tint from a reef tank. Activated carbon, a porous form of carbon, is commonly used to absorb this material.[9]

Activated Carbon

Removing dissolved organics will help with biological filtration and increase water clarity.[10] In theory, better clarity will aid light transmission through the water column and improve PAR.

One of the big arguments against using activated carbon on a continual basis is that it removes beneficial trace elements from the water.[11] I have used carbon continuously on all of my tanks and have not seen any negative side effects on my corals. This is purely an observation and not based on any scientific facts. According to Dr. Timothy A. Hovanec, a noted expert in the field, "activated carbon is going to have no effect on the majority of elements found in seawater."[12]

Another knock against using activated carbon is that it is unhealthy for certain fish and can lead to head and lateral line erosion (HLLE). A study conducted by Jay F. Hemdal concludes that hard pelleted carbon did not cause severe HLLE, while the soft, dusty carbon did.[13] If carbon is used, it is best to rinse it well with RO/DI water and use an effective skimmer.

Activated carbon can be used in filter bags located in an area of good flow in the sump, or it can be placed in a media reactor, which is my preferred method as it maximizes effective contact time with the media. When using a reactor it is important to not use too much flow, which can break the media up into tiny particles.

The amount of carbon needed will vary depending on the tank. The general guideline is to use the least amount necessary. Over time carbon will lose its ability to absorb materials so it will have to be replaced on a regular basis. Each tank is different, so the frequency of replacement will vary.

Do the benefits outweigh the minuses when using activated carbon? I am a SPS guy and will continue to use carbon on a regular basis, since it improves water clarity. HLLE disease is certainly a downside but following the guidelines of use mentioned above will minimize the chances of it occurring.

Chillers

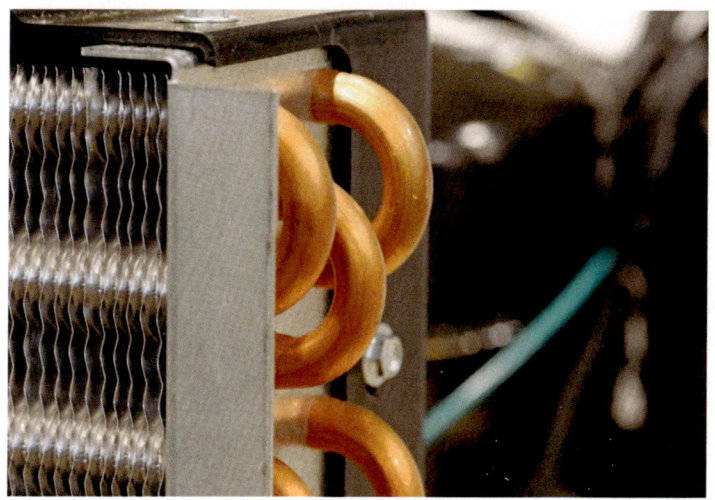

Inside a Tradewind Super 1/2 HP Inline Chiller

There are a lot of variables that can impact the health of a reef tank, and temperature is something that should be watched carefully during the warm summer months. A chiller is the best way to keep things cool, but they are high-ticket items. Budget conscious reef keepers do have options such as using a fan across the top of the tank to promote evaporation, which cools the water. This is exactly what I did when I first entered the hobby fresh out of college with minimal coin. The fans certainly worked but I needed more cooling power and pondered other cheap alternatives. I came up with what I thought was a bright idea at the time, find an old water cooler and turn it into a DIY chiller.

Somehow I was able to track down a working unit that was being thrown out, and I was in business. Or so I thought. Ultimately, I didn't have the technical expertise or patience to make it work, but at least I gave it the old college try. There are other DIY options such as using a dorm fridge, but one should use extreme caution since a homemade device is going to have reliability issues.

Lighting is another thing to consider when pondering whether a chiller is necessary. The metal halides I use are very warm, so using lights that don't emit a lot of heat such as LEDs would certainly help.

The location of tank equipment can also have an impact on temperature. As I mentioned earlier, having a remote sump in a cool area such as a basement will help. If that is not an option, fans inside the stand might be necessary to keep equipment cool.

Personally, I have plunked down the bucks for a chiller for my reef tanks and it has been money well spent. An aquarium can go south in a hurry if things heat up, so having a cooling solution is very important.

Aquarium Controllers

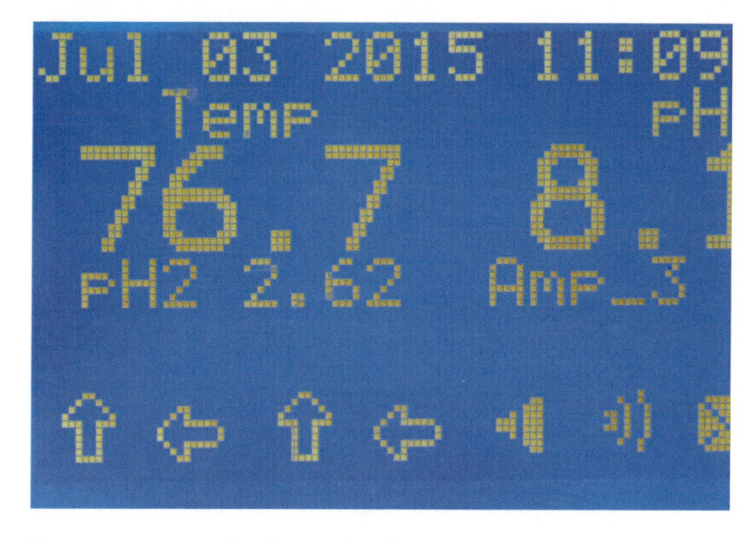

Say you are away for the weekend and set the automatic feeder to keep your fish fed while you're gone. The tank has been running on autopilot for a while now, so you assume everything will be fine while you are away. However, what you don't anticipate is an equipment malfunction with the automatic top-off device. It proceeds to dump excessive amounts of kalkwasser into your sump, elevating pH and killing many of your prized SPS.

This is just one of many possible unforeseen scenarios that can happen while keeping a saltwater reef tank. In this hobby technology is your friend. I consider myself an old-school SPS reef keeper but I don't consider myself old school when it comes to utilizing technology to protect my reef. I have a controller and it provides peace of mind on so many levels.

Neptune Apex Controller

Ph monitoring is especially helpful if you run a calcium reactor. If the c02 regulator goes nuts and dumps too much c02 into the tank, an email and text message is sent to notify the aquarist about a large drop in pH (c02 decreases pH). Furthermore, the controller can shut off the c02 if the pH drops below a certain level set by the user.

My controller will also send me alarms if the temperature is too low or too high, a good indicator that something might be up with the heater.

Water on the floor? Oh boy, that is every reef keeper's fear, but you do want to know sooner then later. I recently purchased a leak detection module for my controller to monitor just that thing.

Neptune Leak Detector Module

A controller can also notify you of power outages and let you know if the water in your sump is too low or too high. As I touched on earlier, it can also prevent a skimmer from overflowing. There are many other programming possibilities, so to me a controller is something every reef keeper should invest in. It's no surrogate for autopilot, but it is close!

CHAPTER 4

Aquascaping

Less is Better

I HAVE TO ADMIT I was clueless when I set out to design my first aquascape with live rock. The "wall" of rock I put together with my first reef, the 90 gallon tank, seemed like a good idea at the time, but the stacked and unstable structure led me to fiddle with it numerous times, trying my patience and upsetting the delicate balance of my reef. At times it looked like a poorly constructed brick wall!

Back in the day (yes I am considered an "old timer" by reef keeping standards), a popular belief was to use 2 lbs of live rock for every gallon of water. I adhered to this philosophy with my next reef, a 120 gallon tank, and used about 250 pounds of rock. My aquascaping talents improved, and I did a better job placing the rock in a much more stable and natural looking reef structure. I put the time in in the beginning to get it "right" and resisted the temptation to tinker thereafter. This worked great for a couple of years, but eventually I ran into trouble as I had overlooked a couple of important things.

One was circulation. As I discussed, strong flow is vital for a reef tank, and the large foundation of rock had restricted flow and created 'dead' spots and detritus traps that aided the buildup of nitrates and phosphates.

Secondly, I didn't give corals enough room to grow. When the rock was placed I was very satisfied about how the tank looked full despite it not having corals. I had fallen victim to the instant gratification syndrome and I didn't even realize it at the time. Anyway, SPS in the tank grew rather quickly and over time it severely limited the circulation and became a breeding ground for problematic algae.

I finally "got it" with my 225 gallon tank. I used approximately 100 lbs of live rock and created two islands, giving the corals plenty of room to grow. To maximize flow in the back I created a large channel between the rock islands and the back panel of the tank.

The Channel Behind Live Rock in My 225 Gallon Reef

I placed two re-circulating pumps, one in each back corner, and had them facing one another, which created a nice surge and helped minimize the amount of detritus that settled in the back, a setup that aided nitrate and phosphate reduction.

The space between the rock and the back wall also gave me easier access to the back panel in order to keep it cleaner, allowing the corals to "pop" against a black piece of acrylic attached to the back glass.

It did take me a while, but over time I came to realize that "less is better" when it comes to creating effective and appealing aquascapes. We are reef keepers, not bricklayers!

Dry Rock vs Live Rock – Which One to Choose?

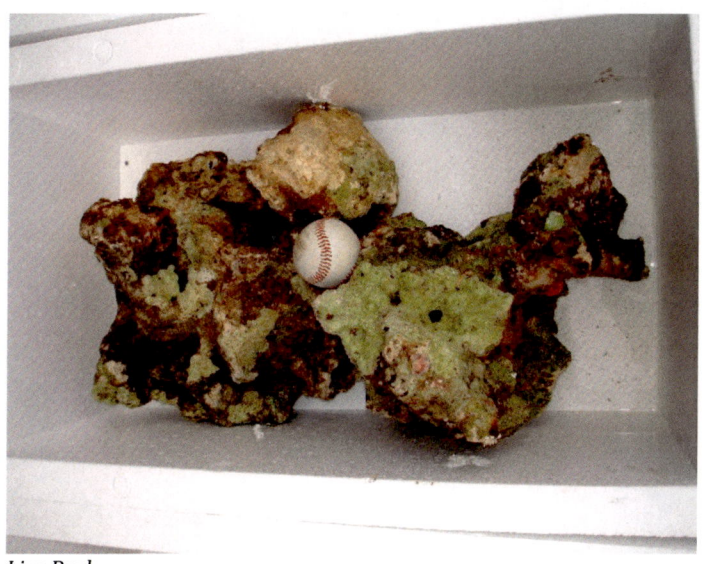

Live Rock

Up until recently, I had always used live rock to start my reef tanks. So why did I use 100% dry rock to start my latest reef? Here is my rationale.

Let's start by looking at the pros and cons of each. Fully cured live rock comes with a lot of biodiversity, and is a great way to cycle a tank quickly. Some just prefer that instant, natural look and are intrigued by what can appear or emerge over time. I always got jazzed when I started a new tank, as I really enjoyed studying the nooks and crannies of the rock for new "life".

Live rock can also come with coralline algae, which is beneficial since it adds color to the reef scape and prevents problematic algae from taking hold. Coralline also acts as glue to hold pieces of rock together, providing stability to the reef. It is possible to add coralline to dry rock but it will take a while. Options for this practice include using coralline scrapings from another tank, or purchasing a commercial starter kit.

The big downside for me regarding live rock is the potential for hitchhikers. You never know what lies inside, so there is always the possibility of importing an unwanted critter such as a mantis shrimp or crab with an appetite for SPS. I never had to deal with a mantis shrimp but I did have to hunt down and catch a number of naughty crabs (they always seemed to have red eyes!), not an easy task to say the least.

Anemones such as Aptasia or Majano can also be attached to live rock and cause major problems, given their ability to spread quickly and overtake an entire reef. Problematic algae such as bryopsis is another potential hitch hiker.

I do want to point out that all of the hitch hikers mentioned can also make their way into a dry rock tank if corals added to the tank are attached to a piece of live rock with a resident hitchhiker. However, the likelihood of having hitchhikers is greatly reduced if only dry rock is used.

Regarding cycling a tank with dry rock, it will typically take longer than it would with live rock (more on this topic in a bit).

An additional downside with dry rock is the possibility that it might leach phosphates into the water and thereby spur on algae growth. One rather extreme way to get around this is to remove the phosphates by giving the rock a bath in an acid solution. You really have to be careful when doing this since this process involves a volatile chemical reaction. I don't think this step is necessary with most rock, so my recommendation is to simply soak the rock a bit in RO/DI water to remove any dust that might clog the filter socks.

Essentially, my overriding fear of hitchhikers is what swayed me to initially go the dry rock route for my latest tank. Having more time to prepare and sculpt the aquascape outside of the tank was also a fun benefit. What's more, dry rock is less expensive.

So how did my dry rock only tank fare? Well, for the first year and a half I had problems that I had never encountered before with my live rock only tanks. I just couldn't grow SPS like I had in the past. First it was a bacterial bloom, and then I had a bad case of diatoms. The biggest problem turned out to be dinoflagellates, an issue that caused me to break the tank down completely, throw out the dry rock and live sand, and start over.

Do I have direct proof the dry rock was the culprit? No, but I do have anecdotal evidence from other veteran reef keepers who'd had similar issues when using dry rock only to start a reef tank. Perhaps my dry rock only tank was too sterile in the beginning and lacked biodiversity, giving unwelcome organisms such as dinoflagellates an open door to dominate and flourish. Nonetheless, I ended up using live rock to reboot my tank.

Sand Bed or Bare Bottom?

There are a number of healthy debates in the world of hobby reef keeping, and one of the more popular ones is whether or not to use a live sand bed in a reef tank. Folks in the bare bottom camp like the fact that they can easily siphon off the detritus that collects on the bottom of the tank, making it easier to export excessive nutrients.

Detritus will also be less likely to collect underneath rockwork in a bare bottom tank where the strong flow required by SPS can flush it out, making it easier to export excesses via mechanical filtration. Adversely, strong flow can create issues in a tank with a sand bed since there is the potential for a sand storm when the current is too strong.

Ok, now lets explore some reasons why it might make sense to use a sand bed. As mentioned earlier, a sand bed provides another home for bacteria in addition to that of live rock, acting as an extra biological filter for the tank. Remember, the bacteria do the heavy lifting when it comes to removing and recycling excess nutrients found in fish and invertebrate waste.

A sand bed also provides a food source for corals and other organisms in reef tanks. The sand bed clean-up crew, consisting of organisms such as bristle worms, sea cucumbers and snails, produce eggs and larvae that find their way into the water column, acting as a food source for SPS and other filter feeding corals.[14]

Sand beds can either be deep or shallow. For arguments sake, let's say a deep sand bed is 3+ inches in depth, while a shallow sand bed is an inch or two deep. Let's further assume that the benefits mentioned above would apply more often to a deep sand bed versus a shallow sand bed. This leads to another debate on whether a deep sand bed, over time, is dangerous. Will toxic substances, such as hydrogen sulfide, that lie at the bottom, leach out and cause harm to the tank's inhabitants?

According to Ron Shimek, a noted biologist who wrote a number of articles on deep sand beds, hydrogen sulfide will not migrate up out of the sand bed and poison the tank. He also believes that manual sifting is not necessary to control detritus accumulation. A good sand sifting crew will do the job.[15]

For many reef keepers the choice between bare bottom versus a sand bed comes down to aesthetics. I like the look of a sand bed and have always kept shallow ones in my reef tanks. I also love to keep wrasses in my tanks, something that is not possible with a bare bottom.

Basically, folks have had success with bare bottoms, deep sand beds and shallow sand beds. There is no right or wrong answer since each type has its merits.

CHAPTER 5

Bringing a Tank to Life

Cycling a Tank – Live Rock

AS I TOUCHED ON in the prior chapter, using fully cured live rock is a great way to cycle a tank quickly since it comes seeded with bacteria.

The key to a very quick cycle with live rock is to minimize the time it is out of water, since any dead or dying matter on live rock can release ammonia during the decaying process, which is very toxic to fish, corals and other organisms. A good population of beneficial bacteria is needed to help neutralize and eliminate the potential ammonia. One species of beneficial bacteria break the ammonia down into nitrite while another species converts the nitrite into nitrate, completing the nitrogen cycle.

Live rock comes both cured and uncured. Cured contains a good population of nitrifying bacteria while uncured has a lot of dead matter on it and needs additional time to be cycled and seeded with nitrifying bacteria.

The Early Stages of My 187 Gallon Reef Tank

Most reefers will choose cured live rock since it provides an easy way to start a tank and is essentially odorless when compared to uncured rock. Of course, if you or your loved ones don't mind the smell of rotten eggs or low tide, then go with uncured rock. I am not that brave, and I'm sure my wife would have me sleep on the couch if I tried to pull that one off!

Ok, speaking of myself, when I decided to reboot my latest tank I had planned to go with cured rock to get my setup back up and running as soon as possible. Unfortunately, live rock is hard to come by in my home state of Vermont, so I had to devise a cost-effective way to have it shipped or otherwise transported to my home. Remember, the longer the live rock is out of the water the more die off will likely occur. Overnight delivery is cost prohibitive, so typically suppliers or online retailers will ship live rock via two day air or three day ground.

Because of the risk of die off, these options were not appealing to me, so I investigated other options. I was planning for an upcoming vacation in Florida, so I started to do an internet search for live rock suppliers in that state. I had heard some great things about Haitian live rock, so I focused on finding a store with ample supply. Fortunately, I found one near the airport I was using for my return flight home, so I touched base with the airline to see if I could check the rocks underneath the plane.

The person I spoke with said it was ok, and the price quote I was given to transport the 120 lbs or so of rock I wanted to bring aboard seemed reasonable. But the best part of this plan was the short amount of time the rocks would be in transit and out of water......only 12 hours!

When I arrived at the store to purchase the rock I was amazed to see a bin full of some incredible pieces. Yes, I had hit the mother lode!

A Beautiful Piece of Haitian Live Rock

I cherry picked 127 lbs of rock and the guys at the store packed them into four different boxes (the price per box would go way up if the weight exceeded 50 lbs). I left the store for the airport and quickly found a skycap when I arrived to help me check in the boxes. The price was $410! Oh boy. I had obviously misunderstood the pricing guidelines given to me over the phone, a big bummer to say the least.

What to do now? After recovering from the shock, I was actually prepared to pay that amount since I was not going to abandon my newfound treasures at the airport. Fortunately, the skycap guy was very helpful (hey, they work for tips) and advised me that it would be cheaper to put the rocks into 2 larger boxes they just so happened to have lying off to the side. Using two boxes versus four cut the price down to $260, a bit easier to swallow.

The two larger boxes did look a little flimsy but I taped them up really good with some Gorilla brand duct tape. I was taking two planes to get home and I did worry a bit about the boxes getting roughed up in transit, but at that point I just had to take my chances.

Luckily both flights were on time and I when arrived at the airport in Vermont I promptly headed over to the baggage claim area. Bags started to appear and I crossed my fingers tightly hoping I would soon be able to claim my boxes. No such luck. I asked an attendant about the missing boxes and they told me to ask the folks at the airline counter. To my relief, the guy at the counter said the boxes made the flight but he warned me they were in rough shape. Hmmm.

A few minutes later he wheeled them out and I was shocked to see the boxes ripped up pretty good. In fact, the top was missing on one box, exposing the rock inside. I did a quick inspection and found a note from the Transportation Security Administration (TSA) inside. Nice, they inspected the contents but didn't feel compelled to re-seal the boxes. However, luck was on my side as there was minimal damage to the rocks themselves.

Picking up my Haitian Live Rock at Airport – A Rough Trip!

With yet another epic journey behind me, I was excited to get the rocks back into water. Before leaving for our trip, I had prepared about 50 gallons of salt water in a 100 gallon Rubbermaid tub. The water was heated, so when I arrived home I placed the rocks directly into the tub and turned on some power heads to circulate the water.

I assumed there would be some die off from the trip (the rocks were actually out of water for 13 hours), so I wanted to keep the rocks in the tub for a week or two to make sure no ammonia was present. In essence, I was anticipating a mini-cycle, and I mapped out a plan to make sure the rock was fully cycled and ready for my tank. Here are the steps I took:

- I did a 50% water change the day after my rocks were placed in the tub. This was done to remove as much dead matter as possible.

- A couple of days later I added approximately 20 gallons of new salt water to the tub.
- Live nitrifying bacteria from a bottle was then added to the tub. Nitrifying bacteria typically grow very slowly, so adding a booster product ups the concentration dramatically and speeds up the process.[16]
- I held off on any water changes for 4 days after additional bacteria were added, giving the bacteria a chance to establish themselves.
- Added a pinch of dry food to the tub on a daily basis to give the bacteria a source of energy.
- Did a 20% water change a week after the rocks were placed in the tub.
- Did another 20% water change a few days later.

Throughout this process I tested for ammonia, nitrite and nitrate. After a couple of days there was no ammonia and just a trace of nitrite. Nitrates were over 100 ppm but dropped to the 25-50 ppm range after a week while nitrites dropped to 0. The multiple water changes were done to lower nitrates, which should ideally be around 25 ppm.

After two weeks everything was ready to go into my display, so I added the rock, the water from the tub, and some additional salt water I had prepared. Levels were tested again to make sure everything was cycled, and a couple of days later I added some fish.

Haitian Live Rock in My Display

Cycling a Tank – Dry Rock

Dry rock is void of any life so you will need to do something to kick start the cycle. When I started with just dry rock I used live bacteria as well as some ammonium chloride to give the bacteria a source of ammonia to grow and multiply. Initially, I tried using dead shrimp from my supermarket as my ammonia source but after a while I realized it would not be enough.

I ended up doing two doses of ammonium chloride to raise my ammonia up enough to initiate the strong cycle I was seeking. Soon after that second dose I began to see ammonia and then a couple of days later it started to drop and nitrites appeared. The bacteria were doing their job and after a few more days the ammonia and nitrites were gone, giving way to nitrates. Overall, this entire process took about two weeks.

As mentioned before, water changes should be suspended to give newly added bacteria a chance to multiply, and it is also a good idea to shut down the skimmer for four days. I would also recommend not cleaning the filter socks until there are detectable nitrates.

Introducing Fish and Corals

New Arrivals

Once a tank is cycled it is time to add a clean up crew and some fish to help along the population of nitrifying bacteria, a practical yet pleasing step since you get to see some actual life in the tank! I recommend starting with hardy fish such as Green Chromis or Damsels.

Next up are corals and step one is to settle on a plan for calcium and alkalinity supplementation. SPS will typically require more supplementation versus LPS (large polyp stony) corals, so either a reliable two-part dosing system or a large enough calcium reactor is needed for an SPS dominated tank.

Green Chromis

I like to start a new tank off with some hardy LPS such as Hammer or Frogspawn corals, but before I do I take some baseline readings of calcium and alkalinity to determine how much supplementation is initially needed.

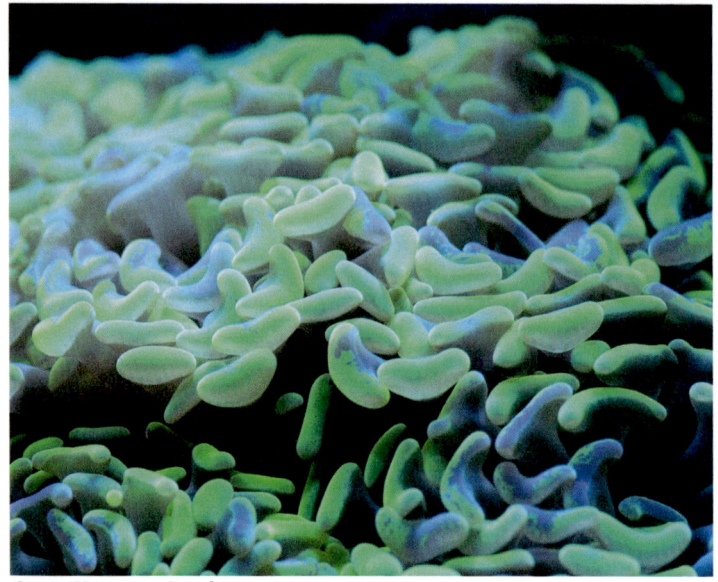

Green Hammer Coral

After adding a few LPS I will monitor my levels closely for the first couple of weeks to make sure the corals are happy, adjusting the calcium and alkalinity additions along the way.

Duncan Coral

If things look good after a few weeks I will add some hardy SPS frags such as Montipora, Stylophora or Birdsnest corals. I delve more into SPS selection and care in subsequent chapters.

Green Stylophora

Time is On Your Side: Go Slow When Adding Livestock

Earlier I discussed how problems can occur when too many fish are added too soon. The same goes for corals. The biological bed needs time to mature, so it is wise to take things slowly.

Another good reason to take it slow in the beginning is to put some time aside to get "a feel for a new system". What does that mean? Well, let me explain with some analogies. I like to bike and a couple of years ago I picked up a new bike and it took time to get comfortable with it. The new bike was better but it was different. I had the same experience recently with a new pair of skis.

There is a learning curve for everything and that applies to reef keeping equipment. For instance, skimmer performance can be dependent on a number of variables.

Bubble King Double Cone 250 Skimmer

What is the optimal water level in the sump for a skimmer? How high up the skimmer neck should the bubble/water line be? Manuals make recommendations but every skimmer is different and requires time to master.

I had another learning curve to overcome with my new media reactors, although it was mostly due to my ignorance (yes, despite being a 25+ year veteran of this hobby, I still make mistakes). The reactors did not come with filter sponges to keep the media in the reactors, so I simply assumed they were not necessary. Big mistake!

After a while, the media (carbon in one reactor and phosphate in the other) began leaking out into the sump and causing all sorts of problems. I ended up draining the sump, cleaning out and scrubbing my three submersible pumps, siphoning media out of the skimmer and pulling out the reactors. It took me three hours, a major pain in the you-know-what.

On the positive side, I was able to pull the reactors out and run the tank without them (while I waited for the filter sponges) because I didn't yet have any corals. This would have been a much harder thing to do if I'd rushed into things and added corals soon after adding the fish. And who knows if all of that cleaning would have stressed out the corals.

As noted earlier, patience is important in this hobby and sometimes you have to make some mistakes before truly understanding its importance. My advice is always to be patient and allow some time to "get a feel" for a new reef tank before rushing to fulfill a grand stocking plan.

CHAPTER 6

Fish Stocking Options

I ADMIT THAT I AM addicted to keeping SPS, but I also get psyched about choosing and raising the fish in my reef tanks. My affection for fish was born long ago, as my father's fish-only tanks inspired me when I was a kid. Picking out fish among the many, many options available is a very personal thing.

Generally, I advocate having a good number of fish for an SPS tank, given the benefits that SPS derive from fish poop. Many reefers believe that fish waste helps with SPS coloration because corals benefit from the nutrients within the waste. I agree with this thinking, although I have no scientific evidence to back it up.

Multibar Angelfish

When thinking about which fish to add, it is important to consider the size of the aquarium. I love Anthias since they are very colorful and can be added in large groups, replicating the shoaling effect one sees in natural reefs. The larger the tank, the easier it will be to keep a school of these fish. Lyretail Anthias are colorful and hardy but fights will result between males and females when they are crowded together in smaller tanks. Typically one male is best, although more are possible when given more space.

Lyretail Anthias

I am also a big fan of having a bunch of Green or Black Axil Chromis and paring them with Anthias. The blue/green florescent color of these fish provides a great contrast to the oranges and purples you see with the Anthias. They also will school, making them a great compliment to Anthias. Again, more success will be achieved when housing these fish in a larger tank.

Lyretail Anthias and Black Axil Chromis

Many fish have unique personalities and number one on my cast of characters is the Flame Hawkfish. Their body is a striking red color, with a black stripe running down their backs. Despite their beautiful coloration, they do look goofy insofar as they are not great swimmers and they have these "bug" eyes that rotate independently of one another.

Flame Hawkfish

There is a certain aura around the Flame Hawkfish that makes them seem more like a pet than your average fish. In fact, my daughter thought it appropriate to give our first one a name, which turned out to be Burt (I guess he looked like a Burt, no offense to any of you Burts out there ☺). All subsequent Flame Hawks I have kept have been named Burt in honor of that first fish and we have never named any other fish, a testament to their funky demeanor. I now have two Flame Hawks and at this point we are calling them Bert and Bertha.

Anyway, these poor swimmers prefer to perch on rocks, corals and anything else they can hang on to for energy conservation. I have to admit I do find it comical to see them "out of breath" when they finally find a landing spot after propelling themselves across the tank.

Flame Hawkfish Giving me The Stink Eye

Angels can be a great addition to a reef but some will nip corals and should be avoided. Those in the Centropyge species, commonly called dwarf or pygmy angels, are known to nip and are a high risk. Angels in the Genicanthus species such as Swallowtail or Bellus Angels are considered reef safe.

Masked Swallowtail Angelfish

The Regal Angelfish is the only member of the genus Pygoplites, and it is a gorgeous fish sought after by many reef keepers.

A Regal's beauty is certainly enticing, but there are a few risks to consider before purchasing this expensive fish. For starters, they are a very difficult to keep and require an established tank of over 100 gallons with a lot of live rock to graze on. It is also imperative to find one that is eating, as this is a sign of good health.

Regal Angelfish

Another big risk or caveat to consider is the Regal's reputation as a coral nipper. Typically, they will not go after SPS, but I would be hesitant to add one to a tank with a lot of SPS frags. A safer bet is to try one in a mature SPS dominated reef.

LPS are another story, as these fish are known to have an appetite for the more fleshy corals such as Acans, Doughnut corals, Candy Canes and Button Corals. They tend to leave Hammer and Frogspawn corals alone, but Regals can mow down Zooanthids and have been known to pick at Clams. I had one in my 225 gallon and it did have a sweet tooth for some of my LPS, although it did leave the SPS alone.

Most wrasses are reef safe and are practical additions to a tank, acting as predators of parasites, including flatworms. My favorites are Leopard Wrasses due to their patterns and coloration.

Black Spotted Leopard Wrasse

African Leopard Wrasse

Wrasses can be tricky to keep, and it is really important to obtain a healthy one that is eating. They also require a sand bed to sleep in, so it is recommend to have sand at least 1-2 inches deep. Wrasses also hunt for small crustaceans and pods, so it really helps to have a good population of these critters living in the live rock and sand. One thing to watch out for, they do have a reputation as jumpers, so carpet surfing is a possibility.

Choati Leopard Wrasse

Tangs are another great option, it is in fact a good idea to always have at least one to keep any algae in check. These fish are herbivores so they should be fed a lot of greens on top of what they graze on in the tank. Some Tangs don't play nice together so it's better to keep more then one in larger tanks.

Many different options do exist when it comes to selecting fish for an SPS dominated reef tank, but it's important to choose wisely and follow certain guidelines to ensure fish and corals can live in harmony with one another.

CHAPTER 7

Choosing and Placing SPS

A REEF TANK IS a growing and evolving ecosystem with many interdependent pieces. One key to keeping an eye-catching SPS dominated reef is to plan ahead and think about what the reef might look like in a year or two when it matures. It's important to do your research and gather knowledge about any corals that you might want to add to the tank. Every reef keeper starts with a blank canvas and the opportunity to create a masterpiece, but certain best practices and tips on choosing and placing SPS can be followed to achieve maximum success.

Understanding and anticipating growth rates and patterns is critical and I can't tell you how many times I've failed to take these factors into consideration. For instance, I love the color and pattern of the Acropora yongei ("Green Bali Slimer") but it grows fast, really fast, and can quickly overtake a significant amount of real estate.

Acropora yongei ("Green Bali Slimer")

The same is true with Birdsnest corals. They can grow like weeds and encroach on other corals, inhibiting their growth. M. capricornus or "Caps" are beautiful, scrolling corals but they are also aggressive and are more suited to the lower part of a tank as they can easily cover other corals that lie beneath.

Orange Capricornis

It is also important to bone up on the lighting and circulation demands of the specific corals being considered for your tank. For instance, a Purple Monster needs a lot of light and good flow and is happiest near the top of a tank. Whereas the Acropora lokani do well near the bottom where there is less flow and light.

Acropora lokani

Purple Monster

The hardiness of a coral is another factor one must consider. More demanding corals such as an ORA Red Planet should only be added after less demanding corals such as Montiporas have established themselves in a new tank.

ORA Red Planet

Another consideration in planning the layout of an SPS tank is whether to start with frags or colonies. Some folks like the instant gratification gained by adding mature colonies, while others prefer starting with small frags and seeing them grow into colonies. My preference is to be patient and to start with frags because they can evolve and grow more organically with the reef, and adapt more easily to the tank's flow and lighting, providing a more natural look.

ORA Joe The Coral

In theory, mature wild colonies will have a tougher time adapting as it may be tough to replicate the conditions where they grew.

Pest prevention is also a big factor when choosing between frags or colonies. The chances of introducing AEFW (Acro Eating Flatworms) with frags are much lower since AEFW eggs are immune to preventative dips and are more likely to be attached to the base of a mature colony or maricultured piece (more on AEFW later).

A frag only display is certainly not for everyone but it can be a very rewarding way to go for those who are patient. Reef keeping is not a sprint, it's a marathon.

Tyree Rainbow Stylo Frag

CHAPTER 8

Mounting & Acclimating SPS Frags

FRAG PLUGS SERVE a great purpose when shipping or displaying frags for potential customers, but they are unsightly when placed in a display tank. I know, over time a healthy frag will encrust and cover a plug, but who wants to stare at that eyesore for months on end.

My solution has been to glue frags to reef rock rubble and then attach the rubble to the main reef rock, thereby eliminating the unsightly plug. The process begins by cutting the frags off of the plugs and then dipping them (more on this process later) in order to prevent any pests from entering the tank. Remember, AEFW eggs are laid at the bases of corals and can survive a preventative dip, so it is important to snip the frag above any part of the frag that has encrusted onto the plug.

Before the dip, I apply a small amount of super glue to tiny pieces of reef rock (aka rubble) and attach each piece of rubble to the top of an empty frag plug. I then superglue the freshly dipped frags to the piece of reef rubble. The plugs sit on top of some egg crate inside a plastic container for 30 minutes, or until the glue has hardened. Then I take the egg crate with the frags and place it at the bottom of the display tank.

Frag Plug

The next step is to acclimate the new frags to the tank's lighting. Typically, frags moving from one tank to another will be under some stress, having been in the dark for a while during transit, so it is wise to allow them time to adjust to the new lighting conditions. An adjustment period also provides a buffer when lighting conditions are different between the new and old tanks, as they commonly are.

For the first couple of days I leave the egg crate at the bottom of the tank and then raise it up about six inches, leaving it there for another two to three days. I don't move it any higher if I have frags that prefer low light. Frags that prefer more intense lighting will be moved up during the next step when frags are permanently mounted.

Freshly Dipped Frags Being Acclimated to Light in Display Tank

Once the acclimation process is over I pull the egg crate out of the display and return it to the plastic container, then carefully detach the reef rubble from the plugs.

I then permanently mount the frags by sticking two-part epoxy to the bottom of the reef rubble and then attach the rubble to the main base rock. Why not use the epoxy to directly attach frags to base rock? Well, when epoxy is mixed together it does emit heat, something that could be harmful to a frag. It is possible to mount freshly cut frags directly to the main base rock with super glue, but this can be tricky as the glue needs to cure a bit in order to be tacky enough to adhere well to the rock.

$500 Efflo Frag in its New Home

Once placed, the next trick is to leave the frags alone. Remember, be patient and let Mother Nature do her thing and avoid re-adjusting the frags.

CHAPTER 9

The Benefits of Keeping a Slightly "Dirty" Tank

EARLIER I TOLD you about my obsession with being neat and how it drives my wife nuts, causing her to constantly complain about my tendency to keep things tidy and in order. She is right. As an example, I do squirm a bit when I see tumbleweeds of hair from our two golden retrievers collect in the corners of our living room. I am the same way when it comes to keeping my fish tank room neat, although I am ok with letting some "dirt" build up within my tank's ecosystem. I think it actually really helps with SPS coloration.

Let me explain. My philosophy is to run a high import/high export type of system in order to maintain a slightly "dirty" tank. On the import side, I feed my many fish heavily, relying on the belief that fish poop helps with SPS coloration. However, I am careful to not overfeed the tank and overload the biological bed. A good clean up crew helps consume any leftovers.

To provide extra nourishment, I will occasionally add certain coral foods to the tank, including feeds from Coral Frenzy and Reef Nutrition.

Oregon Blue Tort (foreground) and Purple Monster (background)

A Well Fed Bangai Cardinalfish

Another option on the import side is to actually dose nitrates, specifically potassium nitrate. Believe it or not, a product used to remove tree stumps, which contains potassium nitrate, is one choice for dosing. Another way to go is to use a product made of pure potassium nitrate.

Potassium Nitrate

A while back I used pure potassium nitrate when the nitrate levels in my 187 gallon reef tank had been on the low side. Over a couple of months I was able to boost levels from 1 ppm to 5 ppm, resulting in noticeably better colors for my SPS.

Ammonium nitrate can also be used to raise nitrates in a tank. A benefit with this element is that it can be extremely pure, unlike other nitrate compounds that often have heavy metals in them, a big reason why I switched to this substance for nitrate supplementation.

No matter which way you go, it is important to take things slowly and raise nitrates gradually. Problematic algae can rear its ugly head if it is done too quickly.

Reef Raft Strawberry Shortcake with Nitrates at 1ppm

Same Reef Raft Strawberry Shortcake a Few Months Later with Nitrates at 5ppm

ReefBum Aquaman Stag with Nitrates at 1ppm

Same ReefBum Aquaman Stag a Few Months Later with Nitrates at 5ppm

On the export side, I rely on regular water changes, heavy protein skimming, a carbon reactor to eliminate the yellow tint from the water, and an algae reactor to remove both phosphates and nitrates (more details on this in a bit). Water changes are key since trace elements are replenished, essential to maximizing SPS health and coloration.

All tanks are different, so it does take time to find the sweet spot in terms of feeding the tank and removing the right amount of waste. But I always like to err on the side of allowing the tank to be a bit more "dirty", even if it does make the neat freak in me squirm a bit. Bacteria in a tank will consume nitrate at a higher rate versus phosphate so I shoot to keep them at a 100:1 ratio, which is the optimal ratio for growing chaetomorpha (chaeto) in my algae reactor.

Ultimately, my goal is to keep nitrates in the 2.5 to 5.0 ppm range, and phosphates between .03 and .05 ppm.

ORA Frogskin

My approach is not the only way to skin this cat. Some hobbyists are successful with ultra low nutrient (ULN) systems in which phosphates and nitrates are kept at or near zero (nitrates between 0-1 ppm and phosphates between 0-.01 ppm). A bio pellet reactor or carbon dosing are commonly used to achieve this nutrient-free state. With this method supplements like amino acids are relied on to feed corals to achieve optimal colors and growth.

CHAPTER 10

Stable Parameters Equals Happy SPS

I HAVE TOUCHED ON this topic a few times but it bears repeating. Stability is really, really important!

I have learned many things while keeping SPS dominated reefs, but at the top of my list is striving to keep things stable. I personally have a hard time with change, and Acropora are the same way. "Stable" is defined in the dictionary as "firmly established, fixed, steadfast, not changing or fluctuating, unvarying, permanent, enduring".[17] For reef keeping, this textbook definition applies to many key measures such as salinity, nitrate, phosphate, magnesium, and calcium. As discussed, keeping alkalinity within an acceptable range is important, but keeping it at a consistent level is vital.

Of course, the textbook definition for "stability" has to be tweaked for certain reef keeping parameters, since we are seeking to maintain established patterns and trying to replicate a sequence of variability. For instance, temperature and pH in our natural reefs around the world will vary depending on the time of day, so consistently mimicking these patterns in our reef tanks is very important.

Acropora lokani

A few years ago I witnessed firsthand how corals can be damaged when a pattern of stability is disrupted. I was away on vacation for nine straight days and had a few people lined up to watch and feed the tank. One of those folks was my wife, who should be granted sainthood for putting up with my reef keeping obsession. Anyway, she was supposed to hit the feed button on my re-circulating pump, but mistakenly hit a button on the light timer that operates two of the three metal halide bulbs. They ended up running for five straight days!

Tyree Pink Dragon

I should have realized what was going on since I was eyeballing the temperature remotely via my aquarium controller. Why, I asked myself, was the temperature not following its normal ups and downs during the day and night? I surmised that we had left the heat on in the house and decided not to worry. I was also monitoring the tank with my dedicated webcam, and all seemed fine.

When I got home it was obvious something was wrong. Several of my SPS colonies had lost some color and appeared burned. Even my prized Black Tang didn't look right, with white patches and what appeared to be scratches on its body. It was stressed from no sleep over five straight days!

Black Tang

This is a dramatic example of what can happen when a pattern of stability gets out of whack, but fortunately the Black Tang and corals recovered (note to self; in the future, look at the webcam when the lights are supposed to be off to make sure they are indeed off!).

CHAPTER 11

AEFW & Red Bugs

PEST PREVENTION PLAYS a huge role in keeping an SPS tank humming along. Just like in our natural oceans, parasites do make their way into our living room reefs. The most well known pests among those who keep SPS are Red Bugs and the aforementioned AEFW. Red Bugs are a nuisance and do impact SPS health, but they are pretty easy to eradicate. AEFW, on the other hand, are a different story, as they can bring a hobbyist to their knees, easily earning their title as public enemy #1!

Prevention

Ideally, the best way to keep Red Bugs and AEFW from entering a tank is to dip any new frags in something that will kill the pests, but not the coral. I use Bayer Advanced Complete Insect Killer. Yep, a garden insecticide! Believe it or not, this product will kill both Red Bugs and the dreaded AEFW. As detailed earlier, this method will work best for frags, but not so well for mature SPS colonies, since AEFW's eggs are likely to be attached to a colony, typically near the base. Unfortunately, the Bayer dip will not kill the eggs.

To prevent AEFW eggs from hitchhiking in on a frag, I recommend cutting the frag off its plug and doing a close visual inspection to make sure it is egg free. A toothbrush can be used to remove any eggs that might still be on the frag after it is cut. I also like to blow on a frag with a turkey baster to see if any AEFW come flying off.

Oregon Blue Tort Frag

I then follow this dipping procedure:

- Acclimate bags containing frags in sump for 15 minutes to equalize the water temperature in the bags.
- Place frags in Bucket 1 and slowly add tank water for 20 minutes to acclimate frags to tank water. When done, remove frag plugs.
- Put on gloves and wear protective eye gear. Bayer insect killer is hazardous to humans.
- Place frags in Bucket 2 with Bayer for 10 minutes. I use a 4% diluted solution, which equates to 10ml of Bayer for 1 cup (237ml) of tank water. I use a small bucket for the dip so in total I use 100ml of Bayer in 10 cups (2,370ml) of tank water.
- Place frags in Bucket 3 with 10 cups of tank water for 15 minutes. Use turkey baster to blow on frags when removing from bucket.
- Place frags in Bucket 4 with 10 cups of tank water for 15 minutes. Use turkey baster to blow on frags when removing from bucket.
- Place frags in Bucket 5 with 10 cups of tank water and glue frags to plugs.
- Place frags in display tank.

This process has worked well for me, and I do believe it is safe. However, certain frags, such as those with smooth skin, are more sensitive and might be better off with a shorter dip. There are risks, given the stress placed on the corals, and it is important to be aware of the potential pitfalls.

Of course, the best solution to prevent these pests from entering a tank is to quarantine them after the dip in a separate aquarium not connected to the display tank.

Managing Outbreaks

Let's start with Red Bugs, the lesser of two evils. If they are found on a couple of colonies it is likely they are on others, so the best course of action is an in-tank treatment using Interceptor, a de-worming medication for dogs. Interceptor is only available by prescription from a veterinarian, so it can be a challenge to obtain. There is one caveat with this treatment: all crustaceans such as shrimp and crabs should be removed from the tank, as Interceptor will kill them as well.

Ok, now let's discuss AEFW. An untreated infestation of AEFW can devastate a tank. There are a couple of options to treat a tank when the little buggers are discovered, so their discovery is certainly not a death sentence. There is an aggressive approach, or a more passive, less invasive method.

The aggressive approach requires removal of all infected SPS from the display and dipping them in something that will kill the invasives, such as Bayer Advanced Complete Insect Killer. A toothbrush will also be needed to scrub off any eggs, as they are immune to the dip. This can be problematic given how difficult it is to spot all the eggs. Furthermore, eggs can still be in the tank if any rocks encrusted with SPS are left behind.

This process must be repeated multiple times over a number of weeks to make sure the AEFW are totally eliminated. Typically, dips are done 1x per week, although some research suggests dipping 2x per week.[18] It's a risky and stressful treatment, given the medication and frequent handling the corals must endure.

I have had success with a much less invasive and passive method, which does not eliminate AEFW but seems to keep them under control. For my 225 gallon tank, I used a turkey baster to blow AEFW off infected corals and into the water column, allowing me to remove them by sucking them into the turkey baster.

Fish can also help during the basting process. I had a pair of Clownfish follow my baster religiously to pick off an easy meal. Wrasses are known to have an appetite for AEFW, so having some of them in the tank can help as well.

True Percula Clownfish on the Prowl for AEFW

If the basting route is taken, it is necessary to be diligent and baste at least once a week. I did lose some corals to the pests when I used the basting method, but the tank still thrived overall, as basting kept the problem in check.

My 225 Gallon Reef Tank with AEFW

CHAPTER 12

Problematic Algae

A Key to Prevention – Excess Nutrient Control

KEEPING EXCESS NUTRIENTS in check, such as nitrates and especially phosphates, will go a long way to preventing outbreaks of problematic algae.

Besides fueling unwanted algae growth, high phosphate levels in a reef tank will stress out corals and invertebrates. Corals suffer because high phosphate levels inhibit calcification. However, some phosphate is required for growth, so stripping out all phosphate is not beneficial either.[19]

There are several ways to control (and remove excess) phosphate in a reef tank. A protein skimmer is one tool for removal, another good reason to employ a strong and efficient skimmer. Regular water changes are another means for exporting phosphates. I change out 10% of my tank water every other week.

Number three on the list is the use of certain calcium and alkalinity supplements such as kalkwasser. As stated before, these supplements not only help to maintain calcium and alkalinity in a reef tank but they also elevate the pH. A higher pH may help to bind phosphate to live rock and substrate, and prevent it from leaching into the water column.[20]

Kalk Reactor

Bio pellets are yet another method used to promote growth of beneficial bacteria that will feed on both nitrates and phosphates.[21] Dosing with a carbon source such, as vodka will yield similar results.

One of the more popular methods of removing phosphates is by the use of GFO (Granular Ferric Oxide) in a reactor. Reactors are typically fed by a pump in the sump, which circulate water through the media in the reactor. A valve is used to regulate the flow rate through the reactor to optimize phosphate removal.

Media Reactors

A fourth method is to set up a refugium and to therein grow macroalgae, a natural method for reducing phosphates. An algae scrubber (a water filtering device which uses light to grow beneficial algae), will serve in a similar capacity, as will an algae reactor.

Which method do I use? Well, for years I used GFO, since it was rather simple to use and did not require a lot of knowledge about water chemistry. Add it to a media reactor, test for phosphates along the way, and replace it when levels begin to rise. Initial equipment costs are low and it is a very efficient means for reducing phosphate.

However, GFO can release impurities into the water and it can also shock corals if it is used too aggressively, something I witnessed first hand a couple of times. Another big knock against GFO is that it not only binds phosphates, but other important trace elements as well. GFO can also be a mess to swap out in a reactor, and it can be difficult to use to target desired phosphate levels. Given these downsides, I ultimately decided to seek out other alternatives. Yes, the time had come to explore a change!

I honed in on finding a more natural means to reduce phosphates and settled on an ARID algae reactor from Pax Bellum (ARID stands for Algae Remediation Illuminated Device). The ARID system exports nutrients by promoting the growth of algae (specifically chaetomorpha) inside a chamber lit by LEDs. The advantage with this system versus a refugium is that the tube and flange design isolates the algae from atmospheric C02. In a refugium the algae is pushing through the water and interacts with atmospheric C02, which can lead to yellow water.

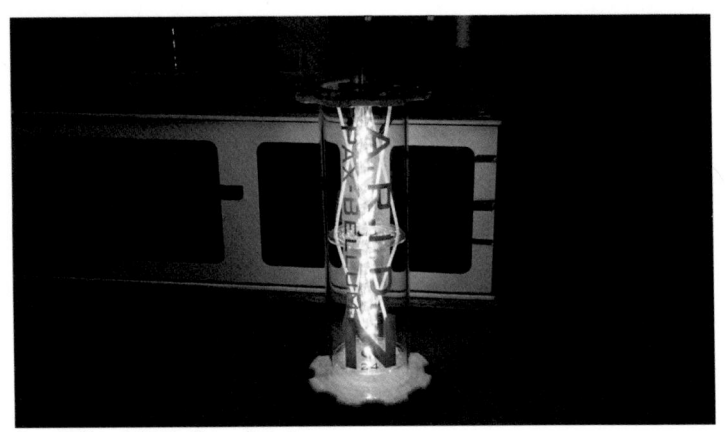

Pax Bellum ARID Algae Reactor

Another benefit of the ARID reactor is it's ability to export both phosphates and nitrates, a plus versus GFO, as GFO targets phosphates only, and allows nitrates to rise. This can be problematic, because a system with GFO can become dependent on the addition of denitrifying bacteria to consume excess nitrate. These bacteria are limited in the amount of nitrate they can consume by available carbon, causing some aquarists to turn to carbon dosing to make up for the deficiency. This can lead to a less stable bacterial system overall, and promote the growth of some undesirable pathogenic bacteria. Not so good.

Here are some other advantages with the ARID system:

- Since the ARID is self-contained, it limits the carbon source for the chaetomorpha to what is respired by the tank's inhabitants, greatly reducing excess organics and making it possible to run a system without a skimmer, or even a sump.
- Can eliminate the need for more frequent water changes if run with the Triton system, which is used to replenish trace elements.
- Ability to control nutrient uptake by ramping up or down photo period.
- No need to repeatedly buy media. Discarded chaetomorpha can be sold, fed to fish or used as compost, something us Vermonters like to do!
- Provides day/night pH stability when run on a reverse light cycle versus the display tank.
- Releases natural amino acids and beneficial compounds into the water.
- Ability to directly take up excess carbon dioxide and phosphate from calcium reactors with an add-on calcium injection assembly.
- Higher and more stable dissolved oxygen levels, a key element consumed by a tank's critters and bacteria.
- Increases water clarity.
- Low energy demand.

Now, the ARID is not going to be for everyone since it will require some knowledge of water chemistry to successfully run the system. Also, you do have to dose nitrates and other trace elements such as iron, manganese and molybdenum, so testing parameters on a regular basis is very important. Additionally, initial equipment costs will be high and you will also have to spend about ten minutes every week or two removing some chaetomorpha and servicing the unit.

Ok, why did I choose an algae reactor versus an algae scrubber? Many folks use scrubbers, but I hesitated since one manufacturer told me I would have to continue using a limited amount of GFO.

Phosphate removal is important, but a reef keeper should be careful to not add fuel to the fire by inadvertently introducing phosphates into a system. Fish food contains a lot of phosphate and adding too much should be considered a primary culprit if phosphate levels are high.

Tap water is also a source of phosphate, so I highly recommend using a RO/DI unit to remove it and other impurities from the water. When using a RO/DI unit it is vital to change out the cartridges when they expire to maintain optimal water quality. A TDS (Total Dissolved Solids) meter monitors water purity and can be used to determine when new cartridges are needed. I always strive to keep my TDS at zero.

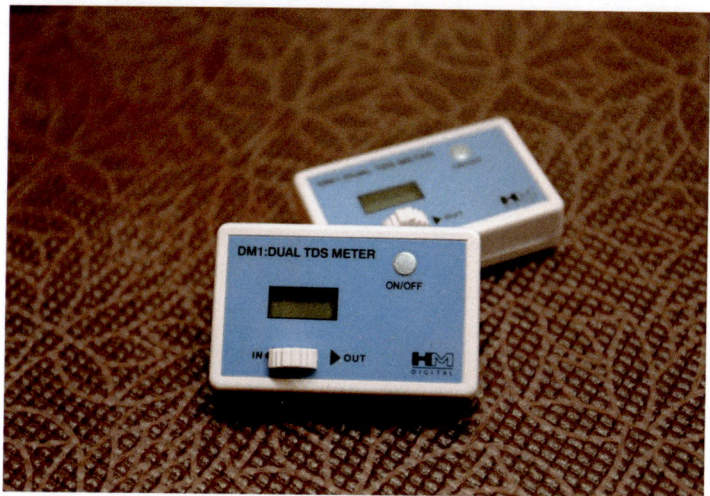

TDS Meters

Another thing to watch out for is phosphate leaching out of certain types of sand and rock, such as dry rock. Lowering phosphate levels in the water column will help to pull phosphate out of the sand and rock, since phosphate levels for the sand and rock will seek to balance with phosphate in the water. Overall, phosphate is very important to reef keeping. Problems can pop up if there is too much, or none at all, so it is very important to monitor in order to find a happy balance.

As for nitrate control, two good methods were touched on before: protein skimming and regular water changes. I use both, plus the algae reactor. Bio pellet reactors and use of a refugium will also work.

55 Gallon Drum Used For Water Changes

Always remember, having strong circulation will also help to keep excess nutrients at bay, as it will prevent any detritus from settling at the bottom of a tank. It is also wise to not overfeed the fish, and to rinse out filter socks and sponges on a regular basis to make sure the biological bed can process all uneaten food and fish waste.

In addition to nitrates and phosphates, algae also rely on iron, silicates and other trace elements to grow. Interestingly, just one of these elements has to be low enough to keep algae at bay, so it shouldn't matter if the other elements are high.

In most instances it is easiest to limit phosphates by using one of the remediation methods discussed.[22]

Dealing With an Outbreak

Creating and running a reef tank is a lot of work, what with all the maintenance and time required to keep corals and fish happy. When things are going well the work might seem minimal or even routine, but when things go south it can be a whole different enchilada. Dealing with problematic algae can be overwhelming and it can overtake its environment in a hurry if nothing is done to stem its growth.

Over the years I have had a couple of episodes with algae that made me want to pull my hair out (I did resist this temptation but Father Time and genetics ended up doing the honors ☺).

The incident that stands out most for me was when I battled with an invasive species of macro algae that came in on some live rock. As discussed, this is less likely to happen when using dry rock.

Anyway, this form of algae had feeder roots that just got into every nook and cranny of my rock. It also formed around the bases of my corals and found its way into the branches. I would spend hours some days pulling this stuff out and removing and scrubbing the rock. I was fighting a losing battle, so I eventually decided to shut the tank down and take a break from the hobby for a while.

Another form of algae I have dealt with in the past is bryopsis. Many reef keepers have battled bryopsis at one point in time and it can be extremely frustrating to eradicate. Manual removal is one way to keep it at bay, but it won't solve the problem. One of the most well known solutions for elimination is to raise magnesium levels in the tank. Kent Tech M is a product one can use for this purpose, but it is important to follow the directions and to raise magnesium levels on a gradual basis.

Cyano is another common pest that can rear its ugly head when excess nutrients are present. It is often referred to as a form of algae but it is actually a bacteria (cyano is short for cyanobacteria).

Cyanobacteria

The best remedy is to increase flow, siphon out what you can, abide by the rules for nutrient control by performing regular water changes, use a good skimmer, avoid overfeeding the tank, have a good clean up crew, and to remove any detritus that might collect in the tank or sump.

Cyano rely on light, as they are photosynthetic, so in extreme cases the tank lights can be turned off for three days to eradicate a bloom. If this option is chosen, one should siphon out as much cyano as possible before the blackout and do a large water change right before the lights go back on. Keep in mind that cyano can return if good nutrient control is not employed and the source of the problem is not addressed.

One other thing to consider related to lighting and cyano is the age of the tank's light bulbs. Cyanobacteria can sprout up under lights that have lost their original color spectrum, so it is important to check the bulbs to make sure they are not too old.[23]

Finally, chemical treatments are another option but they come with large risks, since they can kill beneficial bacteria and potentially cause a tank to crash. I ended up using Chemiclean on my 187 gallon tank due to a particularly nasty outbreak of Spirulina cyano that would not go away despite my best efforts to eliminate it via siphoning and aggressive nutrient control. Keep in mind that this method is just a band-aid and does not address the source of the problem.

Ok, now let's switch gears and discuss another pest; diatoms. Diatoms are a brown algae that typically appear just after a tank cycles, although they can also appear in an established reef tank. They cover just about everything, including sand, rock, pumps and the aquarium walls. Diatoms look ugly, but in most cases they are harmless, so the key is not to panic when they appear.

Diatoms

Diatoms feed off of silicates and also consume dissolved organic compounds, phosphate and nitrates.[24] Unfiltered tap water can contain silicates, and is a good way to jump-start a bloom if it is used to mix salt or to replace evaporated water from the tank. The best way to prevent this from happening is to filter water through a RO/DI unit, although you can still get a diatom bloom when using RO/DI if the cartridge that removes silicates has expired, something I experienced first hand with my 187 gallon tank (one reason why it is critical to consistently monitor the cartridges and replace them when necessary).

Silicates can also make their way into a tank via additives, salt mixes and even sand not meant for aquarium use. The key here is to find the source and to eliminate it. If not, then the diatoms will continue to reappear.

When a bloom is out of control it may be necessary to remove diatoms manually, something I ended up doing to combat the major outbreak in my tank. I used a homemade suction-like device to pull the really large clumps from the rock and I also added a couple of dozen Astrea Turbo snails to help mow down what remained (Trochus snails are a good option as well). Both methods worked to a certain degree, but to really knock out the problem I did a three day black-out of the lights.

Going dark for three days took the diatoms out at their knees. 99% of the diatoms were gone after this period and the 1% that remained were in a weakened state, making it much easier to remove them manually. I admit this was a radical step but felt it was necessary due to the severity of the bloom.

One obvious question is whether this procedure will hurt corals. Keep in mind that there are natural "black out" periods occurring over a period of days in our natural reefs during storms so, in theory, corals are used to this sort of thing. Corals can also be in the dark for up to a couple of days when they are being shipped.

How did my corals fare? Well, all of my SPS frags made it through the blackout just fine, although a couple of pieces exhibited some slight color loss. This was not unexpected since frags are more prone to sudden changes in the system versus full grown colonies. The LPS corals actually looked better after the blackout, with greater polyp extension on my Hammer and Frogspawn corals. My only causality was a small black and white Maxima clam.

I do advocate caution when trying this method. It is a good idea to observe the tank during the blackout to make sure corals are not reacting badly, and it is also wise to slowly acclimate the corals back to the tank lights. I have both T5s and metal halides, so I turned on just the T5s the first day after the blackout, and then re-introduced the halides the following day.

As I touched on, diatoms are typically harmless to a captive reef and can be beaten once their food source expires. Once the kibosh is put on the source, the outbreak should last a couple of weeks, so some patience (that word again;) is required.

A far worse adversary is dinoflagellates. Oh boy, in my 25+ years keeping reef tanks I figured I had seen it all. Well, this can be a humbling hobby and I was reminded of this when I discovered dinos in my 187 gallon tank. Dinoflagellates are notoriously difficult to eradicate, causing some aquarists to quit or break down and fully reboot their tanks.

Dinoflagellates

So what are dinoflagellates? There are many forms, but the kind that gives reef keepers fits is a snot-like algae substance that attaches to rocks, sand, power heads, corals and anything else they can latch on to. They are typically brown, long, stringy and have air bubbles. They can literally coat everything, and some varieties can release toxins that are especially harmful to snails.[25] Correct identification is critical when coming up with a treatment plan, and snail die off is one key indicator that the "brown menace" (known also as dinos) is in the house.

Dinoflagellates appeared in my 187 gallon tank after I added too much coral food. I had ramped up the dosage too quickly and within a couple of weeks I started to notice a brown stringy substance on the rocks, as well as on my SPS frags. I was concerned because it caused the polyps on the frags to retract, and when I used a turkey baster to blow off the substance it returned almost immediately. Not good at all.

What to do? One theory to rid a tank of dinoflagellates is to elevate the tank's pH to 8.4 to 8.5.[26] Some folks have reported success with this method, and I did try it for a bit, but had trouble maintaining my pH in that range. One drawback to consider when maintaining a high pH is that it will accelerate calcification, a potential problem since it can potentially seize up return pumps and power heads.

I then decided to try a different route. My plan was to manually remove as much of the dinoflagellates as possible, turn the lights off for three days (yes, that again!), and dose the tank with a 3% solution of hydrogen peroxide on a daily basis. My intent was to follow a typical rule of thumb for hydrogen peroxide by dosing with 1 ml per 10 gallons of aquarium water. Hydrogen peroxide is an oxidizer and it removes electrons from the reactant that it is exposed to.[27] In theory, when it comes in contact with algae, it breaks down, and thereby kills it off.

Did the blackout in conjunction with the hydrogen peroxide dosing eliminate the dreaded dinoflagellates? It did for a few weeks, but the dinos came back after I started to dose with the coral food again. I was dismayed to say the least, but I decided to throw more firepower at the problem. My new plan was to do another three day blackout, double the dosage of hydrogen peroxide (2 mls per 10 gallons of aquarium water), stop dosing coral food for an extended period of time, and cease and desist on water changes for 4 weeks (there is a belief that dinos can feed on certain trace elements present in salt water mixes). Did this work? Nope. ☹

I also tried to lower my nutrients by using GFO aggressively and skimming heavily, but the dinos seemed to get worse. Predictably, my SPS were stressed from all these unusual treatments, as well as having the dinos covering their polyps. It was apparent to me that I would lose them if things didn't change soon, so I tried some riskier approaches.

I decided to use Vibrant Liquid Aquarium Cleaner, which is a bacterial additive meant to consume problematic algae substances, such as dinoflagellates. I hesitated before using Vibrant since I was adding additional bacteria to my tank and had no insight into how it would affect my current bacterial bed. But I was desperate, so I gave it a shot, figuring I had nothing to lose. After dosing for a couple of weeks, the dinos did recede and seemed to disappear, but this led to the nasty Spirulina cyano outbreak I mentioned before. Anyway, they came back.

What to do now? Well, I had heard of some reef keepers having success using Seachem Metroplex, which apparently kept the dinoflagellates from reproducing. Despite these claims, there was no real concrete scientific evidence that this was true and that Metroplex was reef-safe. But I was at my wit's end, so I gave it a shot. Unfortunately, after dosing Metroplex, my dinos kept spreading and I soon started to lose a lot of SPS.

My last ditch effort was to go the "dirty" method and add a lot of pods to the tank, and to also raise nutrients. The theory here is that pods will help to consume dinos while additional nutrients will spur on algae growth, supposedly a plus since the algae would outcompete the dinos by consuming nutrients previously taken in by the dinos. In theory it sounds good, but in my case it didn't work.

As I surveyed my tank with dismay, it was obvious to me that it was time to start over, since my corals had taken a lot of abuse from all the different courses of treatment. The dinos had beaten me this time, but sometimes a reboot is the best course of action.

To make sure the dinos would not return, I broke the tank down and let it sit dry for a couple of weeks. I then filled it up with RO/DI water and ran this through the filtration system for two more weeks. Two months after adding Haitian live rock, fish and corals I began to notice a familiar sight, dinoflagellates.

Many things ran through my head at that point, including disbelief, despair and confusion. How did they get back in? Did they somehow survive the tank breakdown? Did they hitchhike in on some corals?

It was not a very large outbreak but they were present. At that point I decided to stick to natural methods of eradication. No more blackouts, hydrogen peroxide or other chemicals. I focused on dialing in my ARID Algae reactor to maximize chaeto growth and out-compete the dinos. Once that was done I noticed the dinos began to retreat and eventually disappear.

Was the reboot a waste? I don't think so, since so much was out of whack with the tank's critters and bacteria. I also believe the live rock helped, as it had much more biodiversity versus young dry rock.

In general, as mentioned before, the best tactic to fight algae is to figure out the source of an algae problem before attempting to fix it. If you fail to pinpoint the problem, then problematic algae will keep coming back.

Ultimately, multiple options exist to prevent and fight nasty algae outbreaks, so it is very important for any reef keeper to be diligent, and not to despair when confronted with this type of problem. Odds are, it can be beaten. The best solution is to have a good nutrient control plan in place, and to do frequent water testing to nip any potential problems in the bud.

Remember, algae growth is fueled by a few different elements, but only one has to be low enough to prevent growth (usually it is easiest to limit the phosphates). Most importantly, go the natural route for eradication whenever possible.

CHAPTER 13

Husbandry

KEEPING A REEF TANK is not an easy task, given all the elements critical to success. There are calcium reactors, protein skimmers, and other pieces of equipment that must be harmonized to keep a tank in balance. However, achieving this balance will not guarantee prosperity unless a reef keeper takes care of his or her aquarium and practices good husbandry.

It is really important to spend the required time to do tank maintenance. Everyone dreads chores, but it is so critical when it comes to keeping a thriving reef. Think of a reef as a car. Skip a few oil changes or neglect to rotate the tires and performance will inevitably suffer.

My recommendation is to start off by creating a checklist of things that need to be done on a regular basis. I actually create a calendar so I know when I need to do certain things. Change out the carbon in my reactor on the 4th Saturday of the month; check. Swap out the media in my calcium reactor the last weekends of March, June, September and December; check, check, check and check. I put this calendar together for an entire year and it really keeps me organized.

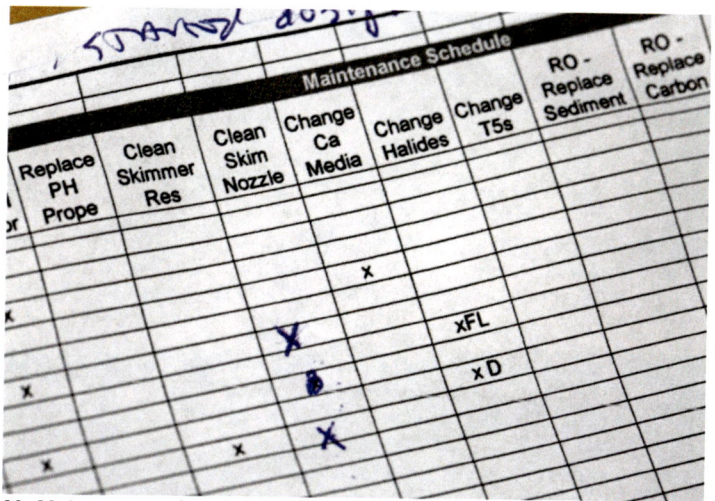

My Maintenance Checklist

Performing regular water changes is one of the most important recurring events on my calendar. The bi-weekly 10% water changes I do add up to a large 20% swap-out over an entire month.

Keeping tabs on water parameters on a regular basis is also critical. I like to test alkalinity on a weekly basis, given how important it is for SPS. I also test weekly for phosphate, to avoid any spikes that might cause an algae outbreak. Remember, one also has to be cautious when lowering high phosphate levels too quickly, potentially causing SPS to fade, so stability is also important for this parameter. Salinity and nitrate are tested once a week, as well as calcium and magnesium. Temperature and pH are monitored on a constant basis.

Salinity Refractometer

Every week I also clean and empty the skimmer cup, rinse the filter socks, and wipe down the light fixtures and the tank's euro-bracing.

Other things on my regular maintenance list include cleaning the glass at least every other day, replacing old light bulbs, swapping out activated carbon, cleaning my algae reactor, and replacing RO/DI cartridges when needed. I also observe my tank on a daily basis to see if I can spot any signs of trouble that might not be revealed by a test kit.

In addition to these "light" chores, it is critical to have a plan in place for some major maintenance tasks. Below is my list.

- Clean all probes in sump every six months, or as needed. The primary precipitate that can coat probes is calcium carbonate. I give these a good scrubbing and soak them in a (1 part water/1 part vinegar) solution if necessary.

- Thoroughly clean out return pumps every three months. I do dread this chore, but it is extremely important since calcium carbonate build-up will impact pump performance. I take my pumps apart and soak all parts in water/vinegar for approximately 1/2 hour.
- Clean skimmer pump and perform light maintenance on skimmer every three months. Stuff can build-up inside the skimmer cylinder/cone at the bottom, so I do clean it out. However, I am careful not to thoroughly clean the upper-half of the cylinder/cone since it could remove the all-important slime coat. Why is this important? Well, new skimmers need to be broken in and typically won't start producing foam in the collection cup for a week or two, until a slime coat builds up inside the cylinder/cone. A good scrubbing can remove this substance, so one does have to be sensitive to this.
- Clean out the sump every week. A LOT of detritus and other things can collect in the sump, so I typically siphon it to suck out all of the undesirables. Otherwise, a detritus trap will form and potentially cause nitrates and phosphates to get out of control.
- Clean out the saltwater make-up reservoir used for water changes 1x per year. I use a 55 gallon drum, and have noticed that certain unwanted residues from the salt mix can settle on the sides and bottom of the drum. My drum is plumbed into my system, but it is easily detachable, making it a breeze to clean.

- Clean heater every three months. Calcium carbonate also collects on heaters, so they need to be cleaned thoroughly to ensure optimal performance.

Major maintenance is super important, and I do sort of cringe when I see it coming up on my reef keeping calendar. However, I do get a gratifying feeling when it is all over and I know my critters really appreciate all of the hard (necessary) work!

CHAPTER 14

Preventing Disasters

ACCORDING TO MURPHY'S LAW "whatever can go wrong, will go wrong". Unfortunately, given the complexity of the hobby, there are a number of things that can go wrong while keeping a reef. Sometimes human error or lack of experience can lead to trouble and throw things out of whack or into disarray. I have certainly made my share of bone-headed mistakes over the years.

Misfortune can also result due to equipment breakdowns or other unforeseen events such as power failures. Fortunately, there are a number of things reef keepers can do to minimize these types of foibles. One thing I like to do, when possible, is to use two return pumps in case one fails. Having a second pump as a potential backup can be a lifesaver when one is traveling and away from the tank for extended periods of time, so it is good to utilize redundancy whenever possible.

Royal Exclusiv Red Dragon Pump – I Use Two on My 187 Gallon Tank

As for power failures, it is always a good idea to think ahead and have a plan in place for when the lights go out. I highly recommend doing this, even in areas where the power rarely goes out. It only takes one extended outage to wipe out a reef, so it is wise to play it safe and be prepared. A full-house backup generator is the best solution, since they turn on automatically as soon as the main power is cut. However, they are pricey, and thus, not a practical option for many.

The second best choice would be a portable generator. You do have to be home to start the generator, but some cost as little as a few hundred dollars and are well worth the investment. One downside to gas powered generators is they have to be refilled during long outages, so it is a good idea to have extra gas containers on hand.

Another option is a propane powered portable generator. I have one hooked into my 100 gallon propane tank, which has enough fuel to power my tank for days. Propane also runs cleaner than gas, and can be more readily available during a crisis, something we Northeasterners learned first hand when a gas shortage developed during Hurricane Sandy.

My Propane Generator

If a generator is not an option, I would recommend purchasing a battery back-up, to power a re-circulating pump during an outage. This setup will help to circulate oxygen and increase gas exchange within the main display tank.

As detailed earlier, aquarium controllers are also an excellent way to monitor a tank and to stay on top of problems before they mushroom into real trouble. For additional peace of mind, I use webcams in conjunction with my controller to provide a visual, should a problem occur.

The Live HD Webcam for My 187 Gallon Display Tank

I like to have webcams trained on both my display tank and sump. One time I used them to check on a power outage alert I received from my controller. At the time, I did have a full-house back-up generator, but I noticed through the webcams that my return pumps were not running. I was able to resolve the problem by using the controller to reset the pumps by switching them off and then back on (it took the generator about 15 seconds to kick in, creating some back-suction, and thereby preventing the pumps from running).

As touched on in the prior chapter, an excellent way to avert any trouble is to keep up with equipment maintenance to make sure pumps and other items will not break down.

Not all problems can be prevented, but certain issues can be avoided by being proactive and planning for some worst-case scenarios. As they say, an ounce of prevention is worth a pound of cure.

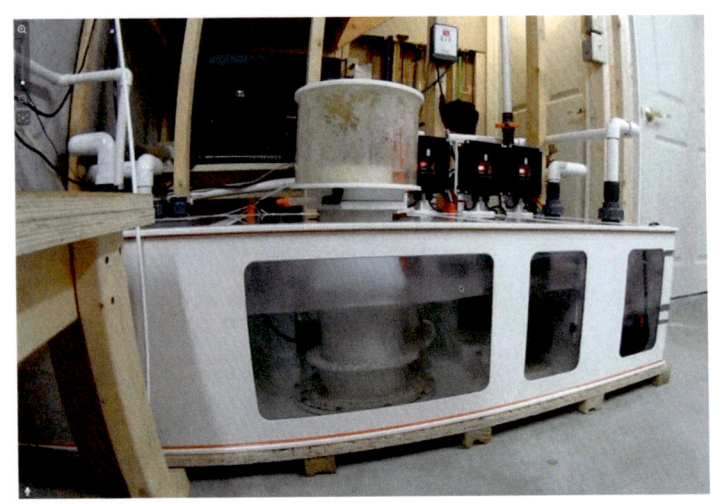

My Sump Cam

CHAPTER 15

Photography

OK, UP TO THIS point I have been discussing best practices on how to keep a thriving SPS dominated reef tank. If you have read this far and plan to successfully employ some of these methods, then you will want to share your awesome reef with others, right? Now, let's talk photography.

General Tips on Photographing Reef Tanks

Reef keeping does require a well-honed skill set, and it takes an additional set of skills to take really good pictures of a tank with a DSLR (digital single-lens reflex) camera.

There are some basic things one should do before even turning the camera on. Number one; use a tripod to keep the camera steady and to reduce shake. A steady hand helps, but any close-up or macro shots will be impacted by even the slightest shake.

Number two; to minimize reflections from the glass, it helps to turn off any lights in the room and close any window shades if photos are taken during the day (taking photos at night is best if the room doesn't have great shades).

A third thing I recommend is turning the pumps off to minimize the movements of corals and their polyps. Lastly, it's important to keep the glass on the front panel of the tank clean and to shoot at right angles to the tank to reduce any possible distortion.

Zooanthids

ORA Hawkins

Acropora lokani

Elegance Coral

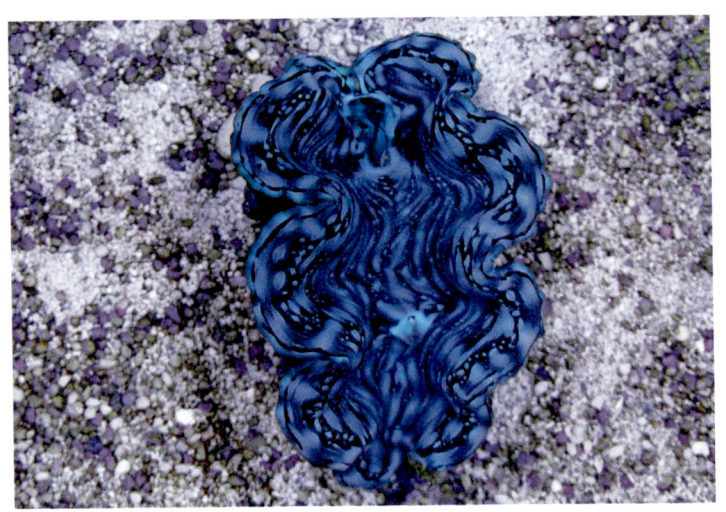

Blue Squamosa Clam

Acropora turaki

Once the camera is turned on, it is always a good idea to set the timer, as a camera can shake even the slightest bit when the shutter button is depressed. It also helps to use the image stabilization option on a camera or lens to optimize clarity.

ORA Pearlberry

As for settings, the best results will be achieved when certain adjustments are made to the camera outside of the preset auto settings. Typically, the white balance has to be adjusted since aquarium lighting can make it difficult for cameras to automatically detect and represent colors accurately. This is especially true if a tank has very blue lighting, as emitted by 20,000k bulbs. It helps to play around with different settings until accurate colors are attained.

Aperture is another setting that comes in handy when taking pictures of coral. The aperture priority mode on a camera enables a user to pick a certain aperture while the camera automatically selects a proper shutter speed to match. The other option is to use the manual setting and adjust both the aperture and speed.

Use of a low aperture (larger f stop number) and low speed will yield greater depth of field for coral shots (more of the foreground and background will be in focus). If polyps are in motion, even slightly, it will be beneficial to go down a bit on the f-stop and use a higher shutter speed to get a sharper image, although some depth of field will be lost. Again, playing around with these settings will reward a shooter with better shots.

Purple Stylophora

Sometimes it helps to adjust the ISO, but one does have to be careful since graininess can result when the ISO is high. I don't play around with the ISO setting a lot, but sometimes it does help to raise it to get a faster shutter speed and a smaller aperture.

Acropora yongei ("Green Bali Slimer")

An Acro Garden

I also recommend an underwater housing for your camera to take submerged, top-down shots. They're not too expensive, and the shots you'll get with them are really cool.

A Top Down "Porthole" Viewer From Avast Marine

Reef Raft Sabertooth – A Top Down Perspective

Tips on Macro Photography For Reef Tanks

Reef keeping is an art form, and this art can be brought to life when using macro photography to expose the rich and infinite details in coral and other reef tank inhabitants. The basic premise of macro photography is to achieve high magnification of the subject. The closer the lens is to the subject, the larger that subject will appear in the image. It is simple in principle, but in reality it can be complicated given the multitude of different options with lenses and settings on a camera.

There are a variety of macro lenses available with focal lengths ranging from 50mm to 200mm. The smaller the focal length, the smaller the working distance between the camera's sensor and the subject. This is important to keep in mind for reef tank photography because the smaller focal length will make it tougher to get close-ups of subject matter in the back of the tank. A focal length on the high end of the scale will provide more versatility in this regard but there is a trade off, since magnification decreases as the working distance increases. A 100mm lens is a good compromise and has worked really well for me over the years.

Don't have the bucks for an expensive macro lens? Then consider using less expensive extension tubes, which fit between the rear mount of the lens and the camera body. Extension tubes make the lens focus closer and thus increase the magnification. You can even use them with a macro lens to get those ultra close up shots.

In regard to settings for macros, I find it beneficial to use the manual or aperture priority modes and select a low aperture for greater depth of field. This is an instance when a higher ISO can be used to obtain a higher f-stop.

When focusing for macro photos it is best to use manual versus auto focus, since a camera's auto focus sensor will struggle to locate a focal point at close range. It is also wise to take advantage of the digital zoom. I temporarily switch my camera to the live video mode and use the 10x digital zoom to make sure my subjects are crisp and clear.

Focus rails can also come in handy when there is a need to fine-tune the focus at very close range, especially when using extension tubes.

WWC Yellow Carolina

Pink Birdsnest

Red & Green Scolymia Coral

Ponape Rainbow

Orange Encrusting Montipora

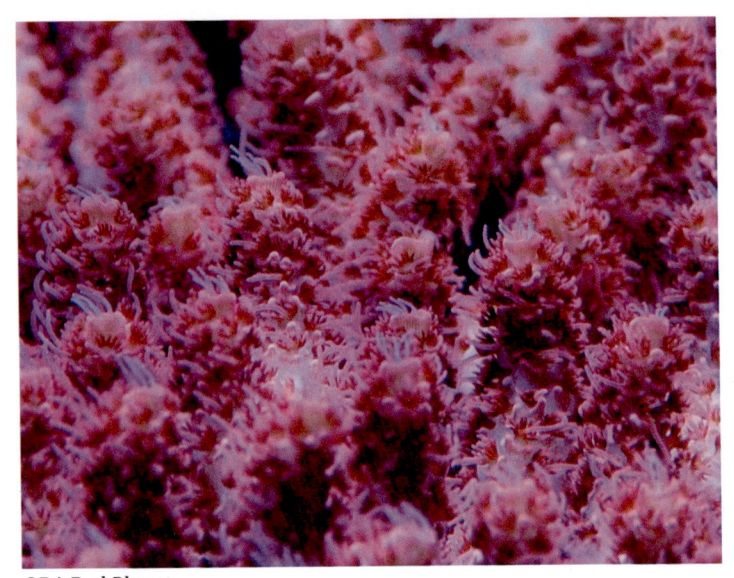

ORA Red Planet

Blue Tort

Reef Raft Pacman Rainbow

Powder Blue Tang

Maxima Clam

Purple & Green Frogspawn

Undata Montipora

Progression Shots

Whether you are shooting macros or something else, have fun with it and document as much as possible. A really cool way to see the progress of a reef is to take progression shots of individual corals or the entire tank. Here are a series of photos taken of my 225 gallon reef over a few years. Where did the rock go?!

April 16th, 2007

June 19th, 2007

August 6th, 2007

October 13th, 2007

December 23rd, 2007

April 20th, 2008

September 13th, 2008

January 24th, 2009

May 1st, 2009

July 15th, 2009

January 30th, 2010

April 24th, 2010

August 15th, 2010

November 13th, 2010

March 19th, 2011

August 21st, 2011

February 28th, 2012

CHAPTER 16

Conclusions – Top 10 Tips

THROUGHOUT THIS BOOK I have touched on a number of variables one should consider when keeping a reef tank, especially one with a lot of SPS. There are many keys to achieving optimal growth rates and colors for SPS but some are more important then others. With that in mind, here are my top 10 tips;

Purple Bonsai Acropora

The List

1. **Stability** - It is critical to have stability for parameters such as salinity, nitrate, magnesium and calcium. Stable phosphate is important as well, but perhaps most important for SPS is keeping alkalinity at a consistent level. Any swings with this parameter over a short period of time usually spells trouble. Stable parameters equals happy SPS.

2. **Proper Lighting** - I have had a lot of success using 400W metal halides, yet others have done well with other types of lighting such as LEDs and T5s. Specifically, my SPS have achieved great color and growth under 20,000K Radiums, which skew towards the blue end of the spectrum and have strong PAR, or intensity. This is a big area for debate in the hobby and the situation is quite fluid given how quickly the LED technology has evolved over the past few years. I did consider LEDs for my latest setup but I decided to stick with halides. Yes, old-school all the way. Hey, if it ain't broke, don't fix it!

3. **Calcium and Alkalinity** - SPS suck up a lot of this stuff, so it is critical to have a very strong calcium and alkalinity supplementation system. I've achieved great results when using a calcium reactor in conjunction with a kalk reactor for additional augmentation. Other reefers use a two part dosing system with great success, and in fact, I am currently using this method on my latest tank. Either way, it is very important to test for calcium and alkalinity on a regular basis. Remember tip #1? Stability is key, especially with alkalinity.

4. **Good Flow** - There are a few reasons why this is important. One is to keep detritus from collecting at the bottom, which helps to keep nitrates and phosphates from building up in the tank. Strong circulation also helps to deliver food and nutrients to corals and helps to prevent problematic algae from taking hold in a tank. Finally, good circulation creates surface agitation, which increases oxygen levels and replicates the light refraction seen in our natural reefs.

5. **Keep a Slightly "Dirty" Tank** - My philosophy is to run a high import/high export type of system and to have some levels of nitrates (2.5 - 5 ppm) and phosphates (.03-.05). On the import side, I keep many fish and feed them a lot to ensure they are fat and happy. On the export side, I lean on regular water changes (10% on a bi-weekly basis) for nutrient control and to replenish trace elements. I also rely on skimming and use an algae reactor.

6. **Patience** - If you don't have any then reef keeping is not for you.

7. **Good Husbandry** – It's important to keep up with maintenance on equipment, perform regular water changes and observe a tank on a daily basis to make sure things are ok. Testing water parameters on a regular basis is also critical. Laziness can be a killer in this hobby.

8. **Knowledge** - Reading articles and books, and conversing with other, more experienced reef keepers to tap into their knowledge base, is crucial. Mistakes will be made, but they can be minimized if the required reef tank homework is done. It is also important to crawl before

one can walk, so my advice is to not jump in right away and go big in terms of tank size and complexity of the system. Get it right with a smaller system, and then use the knowledge gained from that experience to go bigger when the time is right.

9. **Avoid Stress** – Don't be a tinkerer. Constantly dipping one's hands in the tank to rearrange corals can be problematic because oils from the skin can stress out fish and corals. Additionally, corals will become stressed due to the frequent touching and handling. My advice is to sit back, relax, and let Mother Nature do her thing.

10. **Be Prepared** - Curveballs will come at some point, so it's imperative to be prepared for such things as power outages or potential equipment breakdowns (these can be minimized by keeping up with equipment maintenance). It is also important to embrace technology. A good aquarium controller can alert a reef keeper to many potential problems before they snowball into a disaster.

These tips have worked for me but, as I mentioned in the beginning of the book, there are multiple ways to maintain a beautiful SPS reef tank. This is not a cookie-cutter type of hobby where one size fits all. All reefs are unique and reef keepers have many options to create the tank of their dreams. It's a form of self-expression, one of the great things about this awesome pastime of ours.

If you are looking for additional insights and information, you can explore my many reef tank and SPS related articles at https://reefbum.com. And please be sure to check out "ReefBum" on Facebook, Instagram as well as YouTube, where you can see all of my reef tank videos online now as well as my Live HD Webcam.

Happy reef keeping!

References

[1] http://reefkeeping.com/issues/2004-05/rhf/
[2] http://www.reefaquarium.com/2012/the-importance-of-water-flow-and-movement-2/
[3] http://www.reefkeeping.com/issues/2002-06/fm/feature/
[4] http://www.advancedaquarist.com/2003/2/beginner
[5] http://www.reefaquarium.com/2013/do-i-need-a-uv-sterilizer/
[6] http://freshaquarium.about.com/od/aquariumglossary/g/Bacterial-Bloom.htm
[7] http://freshaquarium.about.com/od/aquariumglossary/g/Bacterial-Bloom.htm
[8] http://freshaquarium.about.com/od/aquariumglossary/g/Bacterial-Bloom.htm
[9] http://www.advancedaquarist.com/2003/2/beginner
[10] http://www.drtimsaquatics.com/resources/library-presentations/aquarium-hobby/activated-carbon
[11] http://www.drtimsaquatics.com/resources/library-presentations/aquarium-hobby/activated-carbon
[12] http://www.drtimsaquatics.com/resources/library-presentations/aquarium-hobby/activated-carbon
[13] http://www.advancedaquarist.com/blog/activated-carbon-indicted-in-inducing-head-and-lateral-line-erosion
[14] http://www.ronshimek.com/deep_sand_beds.html
[15] http://www.ronshimek.com/deep_sand_beds.html
[16] http://www.fritzzyme.com/index.php?p=faq&pagename=general
[17] http://www.dictionary.com/browse/stable
[18] https://reefbuilders.com/2015/09/18/insights-eradicating-dreaded-acro-eating-flatworm/
[19] http://reefkeeping.com/issues/2006-09/rhf/
[20] http://reefkeeping.com/issues/2006-09/rhf/
[21] http://www.reefaquarium.com/2012/carbon-dosing-in-laymans-terms/
[22] http://www.reef2reef.com/threads/causes-of-problem-algae.183791/
[23] http://www.reefedition.com/cyanorra-sucker-getting-rid-of-cyanobacteria-algae/
[24] http://www.advancedaquarist.com/2005/5/tips
[25] http://www.advancedaquarist.com/blog/how-i-beat-dinoflagellates-and-the-lessons-i-learned
[26] http://reefkeeping.com/issues/2006-11/rhf/index.php
[27] http://www.reefkeeping.com/issues/2003-12/rhf/feature/

Made in the USA
Lexington, KY
30 September 2018